Catholicism
The Faith
of Our Fathers

Albert J. Nevins, M.M.

Our Sunday Visitor Publishing Division
Our Sunday Visitor, Inc.
Huntington, Indiana 46750

Nihil Obstat: Rev. Harold Bumpus, D.Th.
                  Censor Deputatus

Imprimatur: Msgr. Brendan Muldoon
                  Diocesan Administrator / Sede Vacante
                  April 26, 1995

The nihil obstat and imprimatur are official declarations that a book or pamphlet is free of doctrinal or moral error. No implication is contained therein that those who have granted the nihil obstat and the imprimatur agree with the content, opinions, or statements expressed.

Written in accord with the *Catechism of the Catholic Church*

Contents

(For subjects see index)

Charts

Let us now sing the praises
of famous men,
our ancestors in their
generations.
But these also were godly men,
whose righteous deeds have
not been forgotten.
Their descendants stand by the
covenants;
their children also, for their
sake.
Their bodies are buried in peace,
but their name lives on
generation after
generation.

Sirach 44:1,10,12,14

Introduction

If the foundations are destroyed
what can the righteous do?

Ps 11:3

The title of this book tells the reader what it is about. The subtitle of this book, *The Faith of Our Fathers*, is not original with this author. It was the title of a book published in 1876 by Cardinal James Gibbons of Baltimore. That book was designed to present the teachings of the Catholic faith and correct the lies and misrepresentations that were being spread abroad by the American Protestant Association, the Know-Nothings, the Ku Klux Klan, and other anti-Catholic groups alarmed by the growing number of Catholic immigrants from Europe. The Cardinal chose the title to indicate to the immigrants and their children that they were part of an ancient religious tradition, and the book's aim was to confirm their Catholic beliefs. The Cardinal also wished to indicate to the enemies of the Church that their own ancestors were at one time Catholics and that in attacking the beliefs of Catholics, they were also attacking the beliefs of their own forebears. In its time, *The Faith of Our Fathers* was very successful and well-served its purpose.

Today the Catholic religion, indeed Christianity, is under new attack, sometimes overt but more often subtle and indirect. Not too many years ago the United States could be called a Christian nation. While Christianity still has strengths in many areas, the fact is that the demographic makeup of the country is rapidly changing. Whereas formerly immigration was from Christian Europe, the country now is receiving people from the Near and Far East in considerable numbers, people who add to the mosaic such new religions as Islam, Buddhism, Hinduism, Confucianism, and to a lesser extent a host of minor sects. While these new immigrants may not oppose Christianity, neither do they understand it nor appreciate its role in the forming of America.

The undermining of Christian foundations comes from many sources. Recent years have seen judicial and legislative decisions made with the sole purpose of secularizing the nation. Schools have been told that they must be morally neutral and that prayer, even generic prayer, has no role in educational life. One of the chief sources in undermining Christian roots is the communications industry which, through motion pictures and television and to a lesser extent through books, magazines, and the press, presents a way of life that is devoid of religion. Material designed to attract and titillate the greatest audience panders to base instincts in language and content. The aim often seems to be an attempt to stretch the boundaries of good taste. Problems are not solved from the moral ethics of religion but from self-interest and feel-goodism. Values, at best amoral, are presented to the public hour after hour, day after day, causing a blunting of Christian morality.

What Christians must realize is that their religion is now a countercultural religion; that is, it is now a religion that is the opposite of the lifestyles, values, and assumptions of most Americans. They should not be surprised at this. Jesus told us long ago that the values of the world are not the values of God. The Apostle John had this in mind when he advised the early Christians, "Do not wonder, brethren, that the world hates you" (1 Jn 3:13). John was undoubtedly recalling the night he heard Jesus the Lord say:

> If the world hates you, be aware that it
> hated me before it hated you. If you
> belonged to the world, the world would love
> you as its own. Because you do not belong to
> the world . . . therefore the world hates you.
>
> Jn 15:18-19

It would be a mistake for a Christian not to question and evaluate the principles that direct the actions of the world. In doing so, the Christian will quickly realize that without a foundation of morality, only chaos can follow. To judge the goodness or badness of human action, to distinguish good from evil, one must have some criterion to judge against. For the Christian that is the law of God as made known to us through revelation and the teachings of Jesus Christ.

Christians, then, must not only be ready to defend their beliefs against worldly values but also be prepared to show the validity of their beliefs to the non-believer. To enable the follower of Christ to be able to do this is what this book is about.

Needed: A New Apologetic

There is a branch of theology known as apologetics that is concerned with the defense of the faith. It is a word that can be misunderstood today because its derivative, "apology," has taken on through popular usage a contrary meaning. An apology is a statement expressing regret for a fault or offense. However, in its classical and traditional sense, an apology is a *defense* of something. The word comes from the Greek *apologia* which in turn is composed of two Greek words:

apo = defense
logia = discourse, speech

This book, then, intends to be a book of apologetics, that is, a book in defense of the Christian faith. It will explain those teachings necessary for Catholic belief and explain the rationale for them. It will show that there is a logic to all that has happened from the moment of creation. It is also aimed to equip its readers with the arguments for defense of his or her Catholic beliefs.

It will show that God exists and that by His very nature, He is a creator. God can be known by:

1. Natural reason.
2. His own revelation.

The purpose of this book is to establish that there is a logic to religion and life. Among the propositions it aims to demonstrate are:

1. The existence of God.
2. God as creator of the universe.

3. Human beings are created with an impermanent physical body and a spiritual soul, the latter not being subject to death but destined for eternal life through obeying God's laws.

4. By the abuse of God's gift of free will, our first parents fell into sin.

5. God did not abandon His human creation but chose the Jewish people to be the recipients of His revelation, promising that from them would come a Savior and Redeemer, known as the Messiah, who would restore humanity. This revelation is contained in the Old Testament.

6. At the appointed time, God sent Jesus Christ into the world. Jesus identified Himself with God the Father and revealed to us that the one God is three divine persons: Father, Son, and Holy Spirit. The revelation and teaching of Jesus is found in the New Testament.

7. To make known His teaching and to lead humanity to its destiny, Jesus founded a Church, promised that the Holy Spirit would keep it from error, and promised that He would be with that Church until the end of time.

8. Jesus appointed the Apostles under the leadership of St. Peter to direct and govern that Church, giving them the power to appoint successors.

9. The Church that Jesus founded is known as the Catholic Church, the only Church that goes back to St. Peter and the Apostles in a direct and unbroken line. It is Jesus' desire that all people belong to that Church.

These propositions and others will be developed logically as the book goes forward. Logic is the science of deductive reasoning, each step leading to a contained conclusion. For one with faith, logical development becomes unnecessary. For one whose faith is weak or non-existent, logical development can lead to faith if one remains open to it.

Here and there will be repetition. This is done deliberately because of the importance of the material. It is introduced first as part of a whole and then later treated more extensively.

Finally, we return to the book's subtitle as we close this introduction. Those non-Catholic readers, particularly of European or Near East ancestry, are asked to recall that, at one time, only the Catholic Church existed and that their

Christian ancestors at that time were Catholics. So what will be revealed here is truly the faith of our fathers.

Review Questions

What does "the faith of our fathers" mean?
What is apologetics?
What is the purpose of this book?

Primary Sources Used

The following are the main sources consulted for this work.

Catechism of the Catholic Church. This book is the official source for Catholic teaching and the present work is written in accordance with it. This new catechism (1994) replaces the catechism that came from the Council of Trent in 1566, taking into consideration subsequent papal teaching and with emphasis on the teaching of Vatican Council II.

Vatican Council II: The Conciliar and Post Conciliar Documents (Vol. 1) and *Vatican Council II: More Post Conciliar Documents* (Vol. 2), both edited by Austin Flannery, O.P. (Costello Publishing Company). These two volumes contain all the pertinent documentation resulting from Vatican Council II and are essential for anyone studying the Catholic Church.

Scriptural quotations are taken from both *The Holy Bible: Revised Standard Version*, Catholic Edition, and *The Holy Bible, New Revised Standard Version*, Catholic Edition. The RSV has been reissued by Ignatius Press under the title of *Ignatius Bible*. I make use of this older translation because, in some instances, the current NRSV does violence to translations in order to conform to current fashion. In a number of places another translation is used for clarity or emphasis and will be so noted (see copyright page).

Abbreviations

C	*Catechism of the Catholic Church*
Col	Colossians
1 Cor	First Corinthians
2 Cor	Second Corinthians
Dan	Daniel
Deut	Deuteronomy
Eph	Ephesians
Ex	Exodus
Gn	Genesis
Heb	Hebrews
Is	Isaiah
Jas	James
Jer	Jeremiah
Jn	John
1 Jn	First Epistle of John
Jos	Joshua
Kgs	Kings
Lk	Luke
Mk	Mark
Mt	Matthew
NAB	New American Bible
NSRV	New Standard Revised Version
Phil	Philippians
Ps	Psalms
1 Pt	First Epistle of Peter
2 Pt	Second Epistle of Peter
Rom	Romans
1 Thes	First Thessalonians
1 Tm	1 Timothy
Ti	Titus
v.	verse
vv.	verses

1. God

Can We Know God Exists?

When the castaway Robinson Crusoe was stranded on a desolate island and destined to survive only through his own self-sufficiency, he believed he was the sole inhabitant of that deserted place. Then one day, as he was exploring his harsh environment, he was going along the seashore when he came upon a set of perfect footprints in the sand. He did not say to himself, "Goodness! Look what the wind and tide has made!" No, he reasoned that someone else was on the island and set out and found the man, Friday, who was to become his friend and companion.

Robinson Crusoe used logic to come to his conclusion and as the Catechism tells us, "By natural reason man can know God with certainty" (C 50). Indeed, it is easier to prove that God exists than to prove He does not exist. Scripture realizes this when the psalmist says, only "Fools say in their hearts, 'There is no God' " (Ps 14). Blaise Paschal, the French philosopher, had his own explanation of this verse (Pascal's Wager): To bet on God is one's only chance of winning eternal happiness; to be against God is a sure way of losing it. A wise man makes the safest choice.

Proving the existence of God is not the way of science which concerns itself with natural sense experience, what it can photograph, measure, describe, demonstrate — none of which can be done with the spiritual. The arguments demonstrating that God exists come to us through the intellect by the use of logic, along different routes, but converging to the same conclusion: God exists. These arguments reduce themselves to two subjects: the physical world and the human person, each of which we can observe.

First Cause

There is a law in physics which says, "A body in motion tends to remain in motion and a body at rest tends to remain at rest." When we look at our universe, we see a universe in motion. What started this motion? In 1955 scientists developed the big bang theory. Fifteen or twenty billion years ago, our universe began in a tremendous explosion. Scientists based this on new telescopic findings. When these findings were announced, some scientists mentioned the hand of God in creation as the only explanation for what had occurred.

Everyone has seen dominoes falling down in rapid order. A person sets up thousands on a smooth floor, fashioning intricate patterns that move in and out, back and forth, up and down. When it is all set up, someone knocks the first domino over and then the eye can trace the dominoes falling one after another, through the intricate patterns, until the last domino in the line falls over. If you should start at the last domino and ask why it fell over, the answer would be because the domino before it fell into it. You could go back from the last fallen domino through the entire line until you came to the first domino which was set in motion by the finger of one we could call the *first mover.*

So it is with the universe. We can keep going back and back, but eventually we have to come to the First Mover or First Cause whom we call God. Everything needs an explanation — Robinson Crusoe figuring out what footprints meant or scientists trying to explain the cause of the big bang. Scholars also call this the principle of causality, which simply means that everything which begins to be must have a cause. A farmer knows unless he plants seed in the spring, he will not have a harvest. A manufacturer knows he will not have a product unless he assembles the necessary raw materials and finds workers to put those materials together. So it is with the universe, and the First Cause that began it all we call God.

Argument From Design

If you are ever in the country, go outside on some dark, cloudless night and look up into the heavens with its stars upon stars, contemplating the order and design that exists. Then you will understand the psalmist who exclaims:

> When I behold your heavens, the work of your fingers,
> the moon and the stars which you set in place—

What is man that you should be mindful of him,
or the son of man that you should care for him?

Ps 8:4-5; NAB

The psalmist looking out at the universe sees a great and complicated design and intuitively recognizes that where there is design, there must be a designer. The designer of the universe and all that is in it is the One we call God.

The time we live in has been called the age of the computer. Most of us take computers for granted, yet the computer is the result of many technologies and the work of many scientists. Every computer has to be designed by someone; it just doesn't happen by itself. If someone told you that computers just happened to be, not designed by anyone, you would reject that conclusion as nonsense.

The human mind is greater than any computer because it is the human mind that produced the computer. Year after year the human mind stores thousands upon thousands of bits of information that come to it, makes judgments, composes music and literature, recognizes friend or foe, and is responsible for the thousands of tasks that we call living. Yet if it would be nonsense to deny that a computer has a designer, how much more nonsense would it be to assert that the mind had no designer but simply came to be? All design has a designer, and the designer of the universe and all that is in it we call God.

Contingency

Something is said to be contingent when it depends upon something else for existence. This book is contingent; that is, it does not have to exist. It does exist solely because its author wrote it and a publisher brought it into print. You and I are contingent beings. We did not come into existence through ourselves but by means of our parents. We are contingent because we do not have to be.

In examining this argument, St. Thomas Aquinas concludes, "For that which is possible not to be at some time is not." There was a point in time when the big tree outside the window where I am writing was not, just as there was a point in time when you were not, and before that when your parents were not. In short, everything that exists in this world came about because of something already existing.

We can go back and back and back, but eventually we must come to a *necessary being* that began it all. That necessary being we call God, the Uncaused Cause. In other words, if there is no first cause, there can be no second causes.

Conscience

Cardinal John Newman makes the observation that there is within each person a conscience which speaks with absolute authority, and this could only come from God. Conscience is that act of the intellect by which we judge something to be morally good or bad. While conscience has no voice, there seems to be something within us that tells us to avoid this or do that. When we disobey this "voice" we are reproached, and when we obey, we are made happy and have "a good conscience." Conscience can be ignored and can be dulled by frequent failures to obey it, but it can never be entirely stilled.

Something had to create the conscience that is within us, and that something we call God. Conscience is God's gift to human beings. Animals do not have a conscience, they are guided by instincts which move them to a foregone action. As humans we are of a higher order with an intellect that can choose good or bad. Free will is God's great gift to humanity and also in its way humanity's Achilles' heel. God does not want to force His love on us but does want us to choose Him. He gives each of us free will to choose Him or reject Him. To aid that free will to make the proper choice, God planted within each of us a conscience. Conscience then points to One who watches over us and guides us. This mentor we call God.

While Christian writers point to conscience as a strong proof for the existence of God, the fact of conscience is found in non-Christian religions and even among pagan writers. The great Greek philosopher Aristotle wrote: "From the consciousness of moral obligation which we find implanted in us we reason back to its eternal source — the Infinite and Perfect." Seneca, the pagan Roman philosopher and playwright, observed: "Every man has a judge and observer of all the good and evil that he does. . . . God is near to you, he is with you, he is within you as an observer and guardian both as what is good and what is evil in us." Other pagans such as Socrates and Cicero made similar references to conscience as God's voice present to us. In short, there can be no law without a lawgiver, and that lawgiver is God.

History

An indirect proof for the existence of God is the argument from history. From the time of the earliest recorded history, men and women have had a belief in a Supreme Being. This belief existed in both civilized and uncivilized people. It can be argued that simply because people believe something does not make it necessarily true, but this universal belief is a strong argument to support those that have gone before. Moreover, it is difficult to believe that over history everybody could be wrong.

Thus going back through time, we find a universal belief in God but this is not the only historical proof. From the parting of the Red Sea to enable the Jews to escape the pursuing army of Pharaoh down to our own times, history has recorded miracles that could only be worked by the hand of God. A miracle is an observable happening in the moral or physical order which contravenes natural laws and which cannot be explained by any natural power but only by the power of God. It is opposed to the laws of nature for the dead to return to life or for a person with a terminal disease to make a sudden and total recovery apart from medical care. To set aside the laws of nature is only the province of the One who made that law, namely God.

Sacred Scripture records for us many miraculous doings of God. But miracles have not ended with the final composition of Scripture. Over the centuries the Catholic Church has recorded numerous miracles which have been carefully examined and documented. A good example of these procedures can be found at Lourdes in France. Lourdes is the site of a shrine built to honor the Virgin Mary. In 1858 a fourteen-year-old peasant girl, Bernadette Soubirous, was collecting wood along the bank of a small stream when she met a young woman standing in a natural grotto above the stream. The woman identified herself as the Immaculate Conception and asked that a shrine be built there. It took four years of rigorous examination before the Church gave approval to the Lourdes apparitions and permission to build the shrine.

Today Lourdes is a center of pilgrimage for people from all parts of the world and it has the reputation of being a place where miraculous things occur both spiritually and physically. From the earliest days a medical bureau, staffed by doctors and other skilled medical personnel, was established to examine claims of physical cures by studying the medical history of the cured person, ruling out hysteria or self-suggestion, before declaring the cure to be beyond human explanation.

The validity of Lourdes cures has been attested to by Dr. Alexis Carrel (1873-1944), a French surgeon and biologist, who was on the staff of the Rockefeller Institute in New York. Dr. Carrel's work laid the foundations for today's many heart operations. He discovered a way to suture blood vessels, and he pioneered in transfusions and transplants, even working on an artificial heart. For his discoveries he was awarded the Nobel Prize in Physiology and Medicine. While on a vacation at home in France, although skeptical of what he heard about the new shrine, he decided out of curiosity to visit Lourdes. Because of his reputation, the doctors at Lourdes gave him the freedom of the medical bureau, where he was able to examine records and study cases. One example of what he saw was a woman near death who arrived at Lourdes with an inoperable cancerous tumor. When she emerged from the Lourdes water, the cancer was gone. When Dr. Carrel returned to New York he wrote about this case and others, declaring himself a firm believer in the miracles of Lourdes.

Another way of knowing about the existence of God is through God's own revelation of Himself. We have been speaking of God revealing Himself to us through nature, causality, motion, and so on. But God has also made direct personal revelation to humanity, even telling us His Name. This direct revelation will be treated in another part of this book.

A final argument for the existence of God is in Jesus Christ Himself. Jesus declared Himself to be God. If this claim is true, then God exists. Further on in this book, this claim of Jesus will be shown to be true; for now, it is merely a statement of proof.

There are other arguments for the existence of God put forth by theologians, philosophers, saints, and ordinary writers, but these arguments are different ways of restating what has already been said here. However, establishing the existence of God is not the end of the quest — it is only the beginning. The next goal of the journey is to determine who God is.

The *Catechism of the Catholic Church* speaks on each of these proofs for the existence of God in its chapter entitled "Man's Capacity for God," sections 27-50.

Review Questions

Can we know from reason that God exists?
Is this knowledge scientific or logical?
What is the First Cause argument?
Explain the argument from design.
What is the argument from contingency?
Does the universal conscience tell us anything?
What does history tell us about God?

2. God: His Attributes

The attributes of God are discussed in the *Catechism of the Catholic Church* under the following sections: characteristics 370; goodness 385; love 218-221, truth 214-217; omnipotence 268-278; creator 295-300, 308; holy 2807, 2809.

Who Is God?

This is the billion dollar question and it has no complete answer. *God cannot be defined.* This is because God is infinite, and as humans we are confined by our finite minds and finite vocabularies. We can describe God but not define Him. Every good word that exists can be applied to God but, even then, God goes beyond vocabulary. Each good word that we applied to God would have to be prefixed with the word "all": God is not only good but all-good, not only loving but all-loving, and so on.

This is not to be interpreted that we cannot know God. We are capable of knowing about God as much as our minds can comprehend. There are different ways of knowing about someone. We know a person by what he or she does or says. A person reveals himself or herself to us in what that person does and says. This is called deductive knowledge. We deduce from what a person does or says whether that person is kind or mean, good or bad, wise or silly, polite or rude, happy or gloomy. Thus we can come to know a good deal about God by what He does and what He says to us through revelation. Hence, by the use of our reasons we can determine many things about God, and these we call His *attributes*. What then are some of these attributes?

One. God is one; that is, He exists without parts. If God consisted of parts, that would mean that there would have to be someone else above Him to bring these parts into a whole. But we have shown that God is the First Cause, so He must absolutely be simply one.

Spiritual. From the simplicity of God, we can deduce that He is a spiritual being, that is, not a material being. A material being is subject to change but in God there can be no change. It is difficult for the human mind to understand this concept because we think in images. God is a being, neither man nor woman, but one who embodies both male and female characteristics. Because God is pure spirit, He cannot be visualized. As a result of our paucity of language and our need to visual, we assign masculinity to God and picture Him as a white-bearded elderly man sitting on a throne. He is neither: He is pure spirit.

Infinite. When we describe a person, we say something like "he is a man, 5-feet-9-inches, 160 pounds." But we cannot describe God this way, not only because He is spiritual, but also because He is infinite, beyond measurement. God has no beginning, no end. There are no limitations to God. When we say God is powerful or wise, we mean He is all-powerful and all-wise. Something finite can be improved or it can decay but because God is infinite, He is unchanging.

Omnipotent. Because God is infinite, He is also omnipotent, that is, all-powerful. The word we use for this when we recite the Creed on Sunday is "almighty." The Catechism (269) sums it up this way: "The Holy Scriptures repeatedly confess the *universal* power of God. He is called the 'Mighty One of Jacob,' the 'LORD of hosts,' the 'strong and mighty' one. If God is almighty 'in heaven and on earth,' it is because he made them. Nothing is impossible with God, who disposes his works according to His will. He is Lord of the universe, whose order he established and which remains wholly subject to him and at his disposal."

Creator (C 296-301). God is the only true creator; that is, He alone can create something out of nothing. We speak of people on earth creating — a composer creating a symphony, an architect creating a beautiful building. What these people really do is to take things already existing and arrange them in a way to make something new. As the brave mother says in 2 Maccabees 7:28:

> I beg you, my child, to look at the heaven and the earth and see everything that is in them, and recognize that God did not make

them out of things that existed. And in the same way the human race came into being.

Scripture tells us that God created angels, spiritual, non-corporeal beings like Himself (C 328-336). Angels have intelligence and free will, are immortal, and pass in splendor all material creation, including human beings. The word angel comes to us from the Greek *angelos*, meaning messenger. Angels exist to give glory to God and act as His messengers. Sometime after creation angels had their free will put to a test. What that test was we do not know. One writer has speculated that God allowed the angels to see Jesus in human flesh and some angels out of pride, under the leadership of Satan (also known as Lucifer), refused to bow down to Him. Whatever the test was, some angels failed and were driven from heaven. As Jesus told His disciples, "I watched Satan fall from heaven like a flash of lightning" (Lk 10:18). Later when God created human life, He put the first humans to a test of their free will and the Bible relates their failure under the temptation of Satan, causing original sin to enter the world. Why God permits Satan to tempt us and lead many astray, we do not know. Perhaps He uses Satan as a means of our own testing. Despite the presence of evil in the world, Scripture (Rom 8:28) tells us: "We know that all things work together for good for those who love God" (cf. C 395).

Since God is all-perfect and in need of nothing, the question arises, "Why would God create us?" The answer could well lie in St. John's inspired description of God: "God is love" (1 Jn 4:8). St. Thomas Aquinas, the great theologian and philosopher, wrote a long description of the qualities of love. Among them he cited that love wants to share, love wants to be with the one loved, and love wants good for the object loved — including the supreme good, God. God being all-goodness wants to share His life, and so He created first spiritual beings like Himself, and then human beings like ourselves. But love demands a return of love, a love that has to be given freely and not compelled. So God created angels and humans with free will so that they could freely choose Him. Some angels and some humans have used the gift of free will to reject God.

The angelic choice was irrevocable, but human beings, due to the sacrifice of Jesus Christ, have the ability to repent. As St. John Damascene observes: "There is no repentance for angels after their fall, just as there is no repentance for men after death" (C 393).

There are many other attributes of God, but the ones mentioned above are primary ones which differ God from all others. These attributes are important because they reveal God to us as He is and enable us to better understand and know Him. But beyond these attributes there are two other ways we can come to know God. These ways which will be discussed later are:

1. God's own revelation of Himself through Scripture.
2. The revelation of God in Jesus Christ.

The Name of God (C 206-209)

When we meet someone for the first time, the polite thing to do is to introduce ourselves by giving our name. The person we are meeting responds by giving his or her name in return. Our name explains exactly who we are, setting us off from all the other people in the world. By giving our name, we make our meeting personal and again when we meet, we know each other.

While God appears under different names in the Bible, He has revealed His name to us. The first recorded revelation is when He called on Moses to lead the Jews from Egyptian captivity, as recorded in the third chapter of the Book of Exodus. After Moses killed an Egyptian who was beating Jews, he fled to Midian where he married and tended his father-in-law's flocks. One day he was with these flocks on the slopes of Mt. Horeb when he saw a bush on fire. Despite the flames, the bush was not being consumed. Moses went closer to examine this marvel when God spoke to him out of the fire, telling Moses he was to return to Egypt and lead the Israelites from captivity. Moses asked the name of the One sending him to the Israelites, so that he could tell them.

God replied to Moses, "I AM WHO I AM." And He said, "Say this to the people of Israel, 'I AM has sent me to you.' "

This name in Hebrew is *YHWH*, which is rendered Yahweh for easy pronunciation. It was a sacred name to the people of Israel, so sacred that they would neither write it nor pronounce it. Instead they called God *Adonai*, meaning Lord (*Kyrios* in Greek).

It is important to note that Jesus used this name of Yahweh for Himself. One day in debating with Jewish leaders, He observed, "Your ancestor Abraham rejoiced that he would see my day. . . ." A Jew replied scornfully, "You are not yet fifty years old, and have you seen Abraham?" Jesus replied, "Very truly, I tell you, before Abraham was, I AM." The Jews realized Jesus was claiming to be God and wanted to stone Him to death for blasphemy but He escaped (Jn 8:56-59).

Jesus in the same debate with Jews warned them, "For if you do not believe that I AM, you will die in your sins" (Jn 8:24; NAB). A little later He predicted His death by crucifixion and told the Jews: "When you lift up the Son of Man, then you will realize that I AM" (Jn 8:28; NAB). Some who heard this triple affirmation came to believe in Him but for most of the Jewish religious establishment, His remarks were regarded as blasphemy, making Himself equal to God, and for that they sought His death.

Review Questions

Is God defined or described? Explain.
Name and describe four attributes of God.
Why did God create?
With whom did God first share His life?
What are some marks of true love?
What is God's name and what does it mean?
Did Jesus ever use this name for Himself?

3. God Reveals Himself

We have seen that through deductive reasoning we can arrive at the existence of God. We have also seen that with the knowledge of His existence, we can also deduce certain qualities or characteristics of God. However, human reason can only go so far. So that we may more fully understand Him, God has revealed Himself to us, the account of which is preserved for us in Sacred Scripture, or as it is more popularly known, the Bible. The word "Bible" comes to us from the Greek *biblia*, which simply means "the Books."

The Bible is the collection of those writings which were inspired by God through the action of the Holy Spirit (C 105). Despite what some think, God did not dictate the books of the Bible word-for-word as an executive dictates to his or her secretary. Instead He inspired men of different times and places to make use of their own skills and faculties to record those truths that He wanted to make known for our salvation and as such He is regarded as the author and the human factor as the scribe.

> Since therefore all that the inspired authors or sacred writers affirm should be regarded as affirmed by the Holy Spirit, we must acknowledge that the books of Scripture firmly, faithfully, and without error teach that truth which God, for the sake of our salvation, wished to see confided to the Sacred Scriptures.
>
> C 107; *Dei Verbum*, 11

Christian Scripture consists of two parts — the Old Testament which is also shared with the Jews, and the New Testament which begins with the birth of Jesus Christ. While the Old Testament tells of the development of the Jewish people and their relationship with Yahweh, it also in many ways prefigures events that will take place in the New Testament. In both Testaments God reveals Himself in many and diverse ways, and particularly in the New Testament through Jesus Christ.

God's Revelation to Us

Scripture is the account of God's revelation to us, a revelation that begins with the creation of the world and ends with the death and resurrection of Jesus Christ. There is a unity between the Old Testament and the New. Events in the Old Testament will foreshadow events in the New Testament. For example, many commentators on Scripture see in the sacrifice of Abraham (on which we will shortly comment) a foreshadowing of God's sacrifice of His Son, Jesus Christ. "The Church has always vigorously opposed the idea of rejecting the Old Testament under the pretext that the New has rendered it void. . ." (C 123).

Salvation History

God's revelation was not ended by the sin of Adam and Eve. God promised humanity redemption (C 55) and Scripture is the account of how that redemption was accomplished. This story is called salvation history. The Old Testament is the account of the ancestors of Jesus Christ. It is the history of the Jewish people, their faithfulness to God and their failures. It presents to us God's prophets who will foretell of the Messiah to come. The New Testament is the fulfillment of those prophecies. Not only Jews but all Christians are heirs of the past.

Abraham: Our Father in Faith

Jewish history begins with Abraham, the father of the Jewish people and as Catholics say in Eucharistic Prayer One "our father in faith" (C 59, 762).

In the northern part of the Fertile Crescent, between the Euphrates and Tigris rivers, there lived a man named Abram, wealthy and advanced in years, married but childless. He was a monotheist (a believer in one supreme God), unlike most of those who surrounded him. Abram received a message from God, perhaps in a dream (the Bible is silent on how) in which God tells Abram, "Go from your country and your kindred and your father's house to a land I will show you."

Obediently, Abram gathers his flocks and belongings and with his barren wife, Sarai, leaves security for the unknown. Because he is childless, he also takes with him his nephew Lot and his family. Eventually, Abram and his party arrive in Canaan. For his obedience God makes a covenant with Abram, promising him that he shall be "the ancestor of a multitude of nations." God changes the name Abram (the father [God] is exalted) to Abraham (father of the multitude); Sarai now becomes Sarah. God promises Abraham that Sarah will bear him a son.

And thus it comes to pass. Sarah gives birth to a son, named Isaac. The boy is cherished by his father for through this child Abraham sees God's promise of a great posterity being fulfilled. Then came the second great test. God again speaks to Abraham saying, "Take your son, your only son Isaac, whom you love, and go to the land of Moriah and offer him there as a burnt offering." With great sadness, Abraham obeys. When they reach the spot (now Jerusalem), Abraham and Isaac prepare a large pyre with wood they had brought. Abraham ties up the boy, lays him on the pyre, takes out a knife and is about to stab the boy to death when an angelic voice stays his hand: "Do not lay your hand on the boy or do anything to him; for now I know that you fear God." For this great obedience, God promises once again that Abraham's descendants will be as numerous as the stars in the heavens. Through Isaac, Abraham becomes the father of the all Jewish people and the ancestor of Jesus Christ.

Isaac in turn has two sons — Esau and Jacob. Esau, the oldest, is the natural heir of his father but through a trick Jacob succeeds to the inheritance. At Bethel Jacob has a dream in which God confirms with Jacob the covenant made with his grandfather, Abraham. Jacob has twelve sons, each will be the founder of one of the twelve tribes of Israel. The name "Israel" has two meanings. For his fidelity God renamed Jacob Israel and then the name came to include all of Jacob's descendants, the people of Israel.

Salvation history next turns to the account of one of Jacob's sons, Joseph, the most beloved of his father. Out of jealousy Joseph's brothers sell him into slavery in Egypt, where by natural ability he becomes a high-ranking official in the Egyptian government. When drought and famine devastate the land of Israel, some of Joseph's brothers go to Egypt to buy grain for the starving family. Joseph recognizes his brothers and tricks them into bringing their father to Egypt before he will give them grain. When Jacob (Israel) comes, Joseph reveals himself and there is a happy reunion. The people of Israel remain in Egypt under the protection of Joseph.

Generations pass and the people of Israel are reduced to slavery. They become very numerous and Egyptian authorities order new male children to be put to death. A woman of the tribe of Levi gives birth to a son and in an attempt to save him, puts him in a papyrus basket and sets him among some Nile River reeds where he is found by Pharaoh's daughter who adopts him and names him Moses.

Earlier we recounted God's call to Moses who responded by returning to Egypt and organizing the people to flee. Through the miraculous power of God the Israelites do get away from pursuing Egyptian troops and reach safety in Arabia. They will wander in the wilderness for forty years, fed by miraculous manna (a prefigurement of the Eucharist). During this time Moses is summoned by God to Mt. Sinai where God makes a new covenant with Israel, the basis of which is the Ten Commandments.

Finally the Promised Land is reached. Moses is not allowed to enter it for once having a doubt. He dies looking down on Canaan and after his death the Israelites enter Canaan and make new lives for themselves. Again generations pass. The Israelites are ruled by wise judges but want to be like people around them who are governed by kings. The judge, Samuel, tries to dissuade them but when they insist, he selects a man named Saul to govern them. Saul is a disappointment and failure.

God makes known to Samuel that Saul has lost His favor. Samuel is directed to go to Bethlehem and to the house of Jesse, a devout landowner, and from the sons of Jesse a successor to Saul will be chosen. God's favor falls on David,

Jesse's youngest son, who was a shepherd guarding the flocks of his father. Samuel anoints David with the oil of succession.

David and the Kings of Israel

David is one of the central figures of the Old Testament and the story of his life has been popular reading ever since it was written down. He is a major figure in salvation history because he will be a direct linear ancestor of Jesus Christ. David developed into Israel's greatest king, a man who loved God but who also was subject to human failures. The Bible depicts David as a man of warrior-courage but also as a poet who composed religious songs (psalms) for his lyre, some of which are now part of the Bible. He brought the Ark to Jerusalem, a city he made his capital. He unified Israel, defeated its enemies, and developed the country politically and militarily. David's rule of forty years and that of his son and successor, Solomon, are described in the Second Book of Samuel and the First Book of Kings.

Solomon became celebrated for his wisdom and the continued development of the kingdom, bringing it to great glory. In his early years Solomon was faithful to Yahweh, building the first great temple to the Lord which housed the Ark of the Covenant. But as Solomon aged, the Bible tells us, his foreign wives turned away his heart. He allowed these women to import pagan idols. Solomon lost God's favor and after his death there were continuous rebellions against his son.

What David had built began to fall apart. The kingdom divided and the new kings lost sight of the fact that Israel was the people of Yahweh. These kings who introduced pagan practices were autocratic and under them the people suffered greatly. As a result the people began to hope that the Davidic dynasty would be restored and that God would send a savior to lead them. This hope for a messiah (from the Aramaic word meaning "anointed one," *christos* in Greek from which the word "Christ" comes) grew even stronger when, as punishment, God allowed the people to be taken into Babylonian captivity which was to last seventy years, all during which the people kept alive the hope that they would be restored to Israel.

The Prophets

The post-exilic period became the great age of prophecy. There had been prophets before the exile, but it was after the return of the Jews to Palestine that prophecy came into flower. The line of David no longer ruled and the people yearned for its restoration. Into this void came the prophets (a word from the Greek *prophetes*, meaning "speaker for"). The prophets were speakers for God, revealing to the people those things inspired by the Holy Spirit (C 702). As the Catechism (64) tells us:

> Through the prophets, God forms his people in the hope of salvation, in the expectation of a new and lasting Covenant intended for all. . . . The prophets proclaim a radical redemption of the People of God, purification from all their infidelities, a salvation which will include all the nations.

Each of the prophets tells us the origin of his vocation — a vision given that must be proclaimed, a mission assigned by God. Amos, who does not regard himself as a prophet but only as a man doing God's will, describes himself as "a herdsman, and a dresser of sycamore trees, and the LORD took me from following the flock, and the LORD said to me, 'Go, prophesy to my people Israel' " (Amos 7:14-15). The great prophet Jeremiah, who was called as a youth, tries to avoid the charge by saying, "I do not know how to speak for I am only a youth." God replies to him, "Do not say, 'I am only a youth,' for to all to whom I send you, you shall go, and whatever I command you you shall speak."

There are two ways of looking at the prophets, solely in light of the Old Testament, or through the light of both the Old and New Testament. The people of the Old Testament took the prophecies to mean a restoration of the earthly kingdom of Israel by one from the Davidic line. This was the notion of the Jews in Christ's time and even His followers shared this expectation of a worldly kingdom (Mt 20:20ff). It is an expectation that devout Jews today still await, not realizing that the prophecies have been fulfilled. The Church projects these Old Testament prophecies forward into the New and shows how they relate to Jesus Christ. The Church points out that the salvation promised and hoped for is not only for the Jews but for the peoples of all nations (C 64).

God used the prophets as instruments of salvation history. Since God alone knows the future, the prophets knew nothing from their own knowledge but revealed that which the Holy Spirit inspired them to say. Like John the Baptist they were to prepare the way of the Lord. The prophecies they made about the Messiah were not to be completed in their own time or in the time of the Old Covenant. The fulfillment was to take place in the New Covenant and the one who was to be that completion is Jesus Christ.

Review Questions

From where does the word "Bible" come?

How is the Bible inspired?

Why is the Bible called salvation history?

Why does the Roman Canon (EP I) call Abraham "our father in faith"?

Briefly summarize Jewish history from Abraham to Moses.

Why is David a major figure in salvation history?

What does the word "prophet" mean? What was the prophet's role in salvation history?

4. Jesus Christ: God's Final Revelation

Long ago God spoke to our ancestors in many and various ways
by the prophets, but in these last days he has spoken to us by a
Son, whom he appointed heir of all things. . . . He is the reflection
of God's glory and the exact imprint of God's very being, and he
sustains all things by his powerful word.

Heb 1:1-3

And we have seen and do testify that the Father has sent his Son
as the Savior of the world. God abides in those who confess that
Jesus is the Son of God. . . .

1 Jn 4:14-15

The Church's teaching on Jesus as the final revelation is
beautifully stated in the *Catechism of the Catholic Church* in
sections 65-67. "Christ, the Son of God made man, is the
Father's one, perfect, and unsurpassable Word. In him he has
said everything; there will be no other word than this one" (C
65).

The Prophets Foretell of Jesus Christ

The Old Testament is both a history and a revelation of
expectation. God used His prophets to foreshadow the
Redeemer and Savior who was to come and to give credentials
that would prove the Messiah. In fact, Jesus Himself was the
first to use these Old Testament proofs of His claims. On that
first Easter Sunday two of His followers were returning home
to Emmaus from Jerusalem when they were joined by Jesus,
although as Scripture tells us "their eyes were kept from
recognizing him" (Lk 24:16). The disciples tell the stranger
their grief at the death of Jesus and the end of their hopes.

"Oh, how foolish you are," Jesus exclaims, "and how slow
of heart to believe all that the prophets have declared." Luke
continues his account (Lk 24:27): "Then beginning with Moses
and all the prophets, he interpreted to them the things about
himself in all the scriptures."

Let us examine a few of the "things about himself" that were foretold in Scripture.

The Messiah Would Be Descended From David. Isaiah predicted: "A shoot shall come out from the stump of Jesse, and a branch shall grow out of his roots" (Is 11:1). Jesse was the father of David from whom Judean kings descended. This dynasty will produce a new branch which will be Jesus Christ. Isaiah then goes on to foretell the qualities of the Messiah.

The Messiah Will Be Born in Bethlehem. Micah, the last of the prophets of the eighth century BC, predicted (5:2), "But you, O Bethlehem of Ephrathah, who are one of the little clans of Judah, from you shall come forth for me one who is to rule in Israel, whose origin is from of old, from ancient days." After the conquest of Canaan, Bethlehem was settled by the Ephrathah clan of the tribe of Judah. King Herod will use this prophecy to kill the male children of Bethlehem (Mt 2:1-6; 16-18).

The Messiah Will Be Born of a Virgin Mother. Isaiah predicted (7:14) that "the Lord himself will give you a sign. Look the young woman is with child and shall bear a son, and shall name him Immanuel." The word used for "young woman" is *alma* which the Greek translates as "the virgin" and others translate as "unmarried maiden." The name "Immanuel" means "God Is With Us."

The Messiah Will Be the Son of God. In Psalm 2 on God's Anointed, God speaks of the Messiah (v. 7): "You are my son, today I have begotten you."

Passion and Death of the Messiah. The prophets of the Old Testament give many testimonies related to the suffering and death of Jesus. Zechariah describes the Palm Sunday entrance of Jesus into Jerusalem (9:9): "Rejoice greatly, O daughter of Zion! Shout aloud, O daughter Jerusalem! Lo, your king comes to you; triumphant and victorious is he, humble and riding on a donkey, on a colt, the foal of a donkey." Compare this prophecy with Luke's account (19:29-38) of the entrance of Jesus into Jerusalem on Palm Sunday.

The sufferings and death of Jesus are graphically foretold

in the Suffering Servant prophecies in the latter part of the Book of Isaiah. Jesus will be led to His death "like a lamb that is led to the slaughter" (Is 53:7). Isaiah has the Suffering Servant speak (50:4-7): "I gave my back to those who struck me, and my cheeks to those who pulled out the beard; I did not hide my face from insult and spitting."

Psalm 22 tells of the crucifixion: "A company of evildoers encircle me; they have pierced my hands and my feet — I can count all my bones — they stare and gloat over me; they divide my garments among them, and for my raiment they cast lots." Psalm 69 describes the abandonment of Jesus, the insults He will receive on the Cross where "for my thirst they gave me vinegar to drink." Compare these psalms with the crucifixion accounts of the Gospels.

Victory Prophecies. The Old Testament also speaks of the victory Jesus will win through His sufferings and death. God will set up for Jesus a kingdom that will never be destroyed (Dan 2:44). Jesus will be a light to the nations that God's salvation shall reach to the ends of the earth (Is 49:6).

The Gospels

Before we examine the claims of Jesus Christ as the final revelation, we should look at the authenticity of the source of those claims, namely the Gospels of the New Testament. The Catechism (125) tells us that the "Gospels are the heart of all the Scriptures 'because they are the principal source for the life and teaching of the Incarnate Word, our Savior.' " The Church also affirms (126) the historicity of the Gospels and their faithfulness in handing on what Jesus did and taught. Finally, the Church asserts (135, 138) that the Gospels are the inspired word of God. Let us take a closer look at each of these moral and historical documents.

Gospel of Mark. Scholars are now in general agreement that the Gospel of Mark is the first Gospel that was written and that it was used by both Matthew and Luke in the preparation of their Gospels. The traditional date has placed its composition after the death of Peter, somewhere around AD

65. However, today some scholars have it composed as early as AD 50, or fifteen to twenty years after the death of Jesus.

Mark, also known as John Mark (John being his Jewish name and Mark a Hellenized version of a Latin name), was the son of Mary at whose home the Apostles often stayed and where Jesus may have celebrated the Last Supper (Acts 12:12). Because of his names he is assumed to have been a Hellenist in the Jerusalem community. He was the cousin of Barnabas and through Barnabas became an assistant to St. Paul (Acts 12:25). He is thought by some to be the youth who fled the Jewish police at the arrest of Jesus in the Garden (Mk 14:51-52) since he is the only evangelist to mention this incident. He eventually went to Rome where he was a disciple of St. Peter, and it was through St. Peter's recollections that he wrote his Gospel, as testified to by first- and early second-century sources. This Gospel was written in Rome for a Gentile audience.

Gospel of Matthew. From earliest times this Gospel has been attributed to St. Matthew the Apostle in the list of the Twelve Apostles. He is identified with Levi the tax collector (Mt 9:9-13), who was originally named Levi but had his name changed as did Simon and Nathaniel. It may have been written in Aramaic either in Jerusalem or Antioch for a Jewish audience but only Greek manuscripts remain. Although most scholars believe that it was written after the destruction of Jerusalem by the Romans (AD 70), St. Irenaeus, an early Church Father, makes it contemporary with the preaching of Sts. Peter and Paul in Rome which would date it c. AD 68 or earlier and probably the latter since it was a source for St. Luke.

Gospel of Luke. Christian tradition has always named Luke, the disciple of St. Paul and Paul's "beloved physician" as the author of the third Gospel. Luke was with Paul in Rome and should have come into contact with Mark. Luke is also credited with being the author of Acts and in that book's first verse refers to the earlier book he wrote about Jesus. Luke drew heavily from Mark and Matthew and there are a number of verses in both the Gospel and Acts that attest to Luke's medical background. Luke wrote for the Gentiles, omitting

Semitic words and references found in the other Gospels.
Since the Gospel was written before Acts (which ends with
Paul still under house arrest) and Paul was martyred
sometime between AD 65 and 68 that would place the third
Gospel close to AD 65. If that was the case, it would move
Matthew to approximately AD 60 and Mark c. AD 55 or earlier.

Since the first three Gospels are very similar, covering the
same ground and using the same words of the Lord, they can
be compared in parallel columns called a synopsis, which
explains why these first three Gospels are called Synoptic
Gospels. This does not mean they are exactly the same. An
incident may be reported in only one Gospel or in two of them.
Again, there may be differences in the accounts of the same
event. Some of these differences are due to the author's
arrangement and editorial choices. Others can be due to
varying oral traditions which were consulted. Scholars debate
this synoptic problem even today.

Gospel of John. Christian tradition has unanimously
assigned the fourth Gospel to John the Apostle. The first
written claim that exists of this is in the writing of St.
Irenaeus who tells us that it was written at Ephesus by the
Apostle. He relates that this is based on the teaching of St.
Polycarp, Bishop of Smyrna, who knew St. John. Moreover,
internal evidence of the Gospel as by an eyewitness "whom
Jesus loved" clearly points to John. He was the brother of St.
James and both came from a fishing family, headed by their
father Zebedee. John and James were called Sons of Thunder
by Jesus because of their fiery temperament. John was also
called the Beloved Disciple (also a point of considerable
debate) and, with Peter, was the closest to Christ. He alone of
the Apostles was at the crucifixion of Jesus. After arrest and
exile, he settled in Ephesus where he wrote his Gospel and
Epistles.

From the earliest days Christians have treasured these
inspired accounts of the life of Christ. Archaeologists and
historians have confirmed their authenticity. Pagans also gave
testimony of Jesus. The Roman historian Tacitus (c. AD
56-115) records: "Christ was put to death by the Procurator,
Pontius Pilate, in the reign of Tiberias." The Jewish historian,

Flavius Josephus (AD 37-98) wrote: "There lived about this time Jesus, a wise man, if it be right to call him a man, for he was a doer of marvelous deeds." (Some commentators consider this an interpolation but it is in the extant manuscript.)

The Gospel authors sought to present the honest truth. As Luke tells us at the beginning of his Gospel (1:1-4): "Since many have undertaken to set down an orderly account of the events that have been fulfilled among us, just as they were handed on to us by those who from the beginning were eyewitnesses and servants of the word, I too decided, after investigating everything carefully from the very first, to write an orderly account . . . so that you may know the truth concerning the things about which you have been instructed." Truth was the aim of each Gospel writer.

Review Questions

What is God's final revelation?
What did the prophets foretell about Jesus?
Why are the Gospels "the heart of all Scripture"?
Which are the synoptic Gospels and why are they called that?

The Claims of Jesus Christ (C 430-451)

The Gospels contain the words spoken by and the deeds performed by Jesus. Through these words and deeds Jesus claimed that he was the promised Messiah and that He was the Son of the Father and that He was God. When we read the Gospels we find many, many examples of Jesus making these claims. Indeed, it was because of these claims that He was finally put to death as a blasphemer, one who made Himself God.

Jesus Claimed to Be the Messiah. We have already shown that the people of the Old Testament looked forward to the coming of the Messiah who was both prophesied about and described by the prophets in considerable detail.

At the beginning of His public life, Jesus appeared in the synagogue in Nazareth (Lk 4:16-21). He stood up to read and opened the scroll to a prophesy of Isaiah (Is 61:1-2):

The Spirit of the Lord is upon me,
because he has anointed me to bring
good news to the poor.
He has sent me to proclaim release to the captives
and recovery of sight to the blind,
to let the oppressed go free,
to proclaim the year of the Lord's favor. . . .

Realizing full well that this was a prophecy about the
Messiah, Jesus rolled up the scroll and turning to the people
in the synagogue concluded: "Today this scripture has been
fulfilled in your hearing."

John recounts how one day when Jesus was passing
through Samaria (Jn 4:1-42), He stopped at a well and asked
a Samaritan woman for a drink of water. They fell into a
conversation and Jesus spoke about the new religious age
which was dawning. The woman tells Jesus, "I know the
Messiah is coming. . . . When he comes, he will proclaim all
things to us." Jesus said to her, "I am he, the one who is
speaking to you."

On another occasion (Mt 16:13-17) in the district of
Caesarea Philippi, Jesus asked His disciples what people were
saying about him. They replied that the people were calling
Him a prophet. Then Jesus said to them, "But who do you say
I am?" Peter spoke up, "You are the Messiah, the Son of the
living God." Jesus answered him, "Blessed are you, Simon son
of Jonah! For flesh and blood has not revealed this to you, but
my Father in heaven."

Again after His arrest, Jesus was dragged before the
Jewish leaders. The high priest asked Him directly, "Are you
the Messiah, the son of the Blessed One?" "I am," Jesus
replied, whereupon the high priest tore his garments and
declared Jesus worthy of death.

Jesus Claimed to Be God. From the above and from other
verses to be found in the Gospels, it is evident that Jesus
identified Himself with the promised Messiah, God's legate.
But Jesus went further than this. He not only called Himself
the Son of God, as many references show, but He absolutely
declared that He was God Himself.

One day Jesus was in a debate with Jewish religious leaders and He told them that they should learn the truth He was teaching so that they could be entirely free. He remarked, "Your ancestor Abraham rejoiced that he would see my day. He saw it and was glad." The Jews received this assertion with scorn: "You are not yet fifty years old, and have you seen Abraham?" (Abraham lived two thousand years earlier). Jesus said to them, "Very truly, I tell you, before Abraham was, I am." The Jews knew that this was the name God gave Himself in revealing Himself to Moses and they considered Jesus' reply a blasphemy since He was making Himself God, so they took up rocks to stone Jesus but he slipped away from them.

The Jewish leadership was incensed by this claim of Jesus. On another occasion, when Jesus was walking in the Temple portico some religious leaders verbally attacked Him (Jn 10:31-39) and threatened to stone Him. Jesus asked them for which of His good works did they wish to stone Him? The Jews replied, "It is not for a good work that we are going to stone you, but for blasphemy, because you . . . are making yourself God." Again Jesus escaped.

Toward the end of His life when Jesus was preparing His Apostles for the death that awaited Him, He spoke to them about His Father (Jn 14:8-9). The Apostle Philip interrupted, asking, "Lord, show us the Father. . . ." Jesus replied, "Have I been with you all this time, Philip, and you still do not know me? Whoever has seen me has seen the Father. How can you say, 'Show us the Father'? Do you not believe that I am in the Father and the Father is in me?" Thus did Jesus identify Himself as God.

There was another important revelation to His Apostles. The Apostle Thomas was absent when Jesus appeared to His disciples on the evening of His resurrection. When Thomas was told about the appearance, he refused to believe, saying unless he saw for himself Christ with His wounds, he would be a doubter. A week later Jesus again appeared to His disciples and this time Thomas was present. Jesus asked Thomas to examine His wounds (Jn 20:27-29), saying, "Do not doubt but believe." Thomas exclaimed, "My Lord and my God!" Thus Thomas recognized Jesus as God and Jesus accepted the identification, saying, "Blessed are those who have not seen and yet have come to believe."

Jesus Proved His Claims. It is one thing to claim something and quite another to prove that claim. Ferdinand Magellan believed the world was round and proved that belief by circumnavigating the globe. Jesus claimed divinity and proved that claim. One day some Jewish religious leaders were verbally attacking the claims of Jesus. He replied, "Even though you do not believe me, believe my works" (Jn 10:38). It was through His works that Jesus proved His claims. The Gospels are replete with the miracles worked by Jesus. We will consider a few that point to the divinity of Jesus.

One day Jesus and some disciples were crossing the Sea of Galilee in a boat (Mt 8:23-27). Jesus was sleeping when a storm arose. The winds created big waves which began to swamp the boat. The disciples awoke Jesus with the cry, "We are perishing!" Jesus rebuked the wind and the raging waves; they ceased and there was a calm. A disciple asked the central question: "What sort of man is this, that even the winds and the sea obey him?" The answer is that only the power of God can command nature.

Sin is an offense against God's law and its forgiveness requires the pardon of the One offended. Jesus forgave sins, much to the annoyance of Jewish religious leaders. One day when Jesus was in Capernaum a paralytic was carried to Him (Mt 9:2-6). Jesus told the man, "Your sins are forgiven." Because only God has the power to forgive sin, some scribes who were watching said among themselves, "This man is blaspheming." Knowing their thoughts, Jesus said to the scribes, "Which is easier, to say, 'Your sins are forgiven' or to say, 'Stand up and walk?' " Telling the scribes that He had power to forgive sins, He turned to the paralytic and said, "Stand up, take your bed and go to your home." The cured man stood up, picked up his bed and went home. The crowd watching was filled with awe at this power.

Some of Jesus' miracles were dramatic: walking on water, (Mt 14:22-23), the feeding of thousands (Mk 6:30-44), the forgiveness of the woman taken in adultery (Jn 8:1-11); but the most dramatic of the miracles of Jesus was in restoring the dead to life. There was the young daughter of Jairus, the synagogue leader, who was at the point of death. Jairus asked Jesus to come and lay hands on her. On the way messengers arrived to say the girl had died. Jesus went anyway and raised her to life. There was the incident at Naim (Lk 7:11-17). Jesus was entering the town when He was met by a funeral procession. Learning that the deceased was the only son of a widow, in compassion Jesus turned to the mother and told her not to weep. Then he turned to the bier and said to the corpse, "Young man, I say to you, rise!" The youth sat up and Jesus returned him to his mother.

The most amazing of these life-restoring miracles is that of Jesus' friend Lazarus, the brother of Martha and Mary of Bethany. Jesus was on the eastern side of the Jordan River in the area where John the Baptist had worked when word reached Him that Lazarus was very ill. The message came from His friends, Martha and Mary. Nevertheless, He remained for two more days in the Transjordan area, finally telling His Apostles, "Lazarus is dead. . . . let us go to him." When Jesus arrived at Bethany, He was told that Lazarus had already been in the tomb for four days (Jn 11:17). With Martha and Mary and some mourners, Jesus went to the tomb. He asked that the stone closing the entrance be rolled back. Martha protested, "Lord, already there is a stench because he has been dead four days." Despite this, the stone was removed and Jesus cried out, "Lazarus, come out!" Lazarus, his hands and feet and face wrapped in burial cloths emerged. "Unbind him and let him go," Jesus ordered. When word of this miracle reached the Jewish high priest, he decided that Jesus must be put to death.

The Resurrection of Jesus

Finally, Jesus offered the greatest proof of all in His own resurrection (C 272, 649-655). By the resurrection of Jesus, the Father put His stamp of authenticity on all that Jesus had said and did. "God put (His immeasurable) power in Christ when he raised him from the dead and seated him at his right hand . . . and has made him the head over all things for the Church, which is his body" (Eph 1:20,22).

As the Catechism tells us (649): "As for the Son, he effects his own Resurrection by virtue of his divine power. Jesus announces that the Son of Man will have to suffer much, die, and then rise. Elsewhere he affirms explicitly: 'I lay down my life, that I may take it up again. . . ; I have power to lay it down, and I have power to take it again' " (Jn 10:17-18).

Jesus Predicted His Death and Resurrection. Although the death and arising from the tomb came as a shock to the Apostles, it should not have been so because He had foretold both. One day (Mt 12:38-42) some scribes and Pharisees asked Jesus for a sign (a miracle). Jesus rebuked them, saying the only sign they would get is the sign of Jonah, who spent three days in a whale before emerging. He spoke more directly to His Apostles to prepare them for what was coming. As Mark tells us (8:31): "Then he began to teach them that the Son of Man must undergo great suffering, and be rejected by the elders, the chief priests, and the scribes, and be killed, and after three days rise again."

Finally, when Jesus was going up to Jerusalem for the last time, He took the Twelve aside (Mt 20:17-18) and told them, "See, we are going up to Jerusalem, and the Son of Man will be handed over to the chief priests and scribes, and they will condemn him to death; then they will hand him over to the Gentiles to be mocked and flogged and crucified; and on the third day he will be raised."

The resurrection is, then, the key proof to the life and claims of Jesus Christ. As St. Paul tells the Corinthians (1 Cor 15:14): "If Christ has not been raised, then our proclamation has been in vain and your faith has been in vain." Paul sums up the history of the resurrection (1 Cor 14:3-8) and cites the numbers (more than 500) who saw the risen Jesus. When we read the Book of Acts, we find that the resurrection was central to all apostolic preaching.

Because the resurrection is central to the truth of Christianity, rationalists and enemies of the Church deny it. Rationalists, who have made reason their god, deny what they cannot explain. The enemies of Christianity know that if they admit the validity of the resurrection, they would have to admit the validity of the teachings of Christ, so these people come up with fanciful explanations. Some say that the followers of Jesus suffered from mass hallucination, that they were self-deluded. Because they expected Jesus to rise, they believed He did. However, Scripture shows they did not believe it. On that first Easter morning, the holy women went early to the tomb to complete the burial of Jesus that had been interrupted by the Passover; they expected the body of Jesus to be there. When Mary Magdalene saw the empty tomb, her first thought was that someone had stolen the body. We have also seen how the Apostle Thomas would not accept eyewitness testimony.

The only other explanation these enemies can give is to label the witnesses Paul mentions in Corinthians as liars and deceivers. If one follows this line of reasoning, one would have to conclude that Scripture is false, unhistorical, and not worthy of belief. All should know that one cannot deny the resurrection of Jesus and remain a Christian.

The Revelation of Jesus: the Trinity

Before leaving this section on the revelation of Jesus, mention must be made of another doctrine He revealed to us, one that is also central to Christian belief, and that is the Trinity. Like the resurrection, it too passes common understanding but is believed because Jesus said it is so. While the notion of Trinity was only shadowed in the Old Testament, it came to full fruition in the revelation of the New.

Jesus continually spoke of His Father, particularly in the Gospel of John, which is more concerned with the discourses of Jesus than the synoptics. Jesus is the source of knowledge of the Father, as He says in Matthew (11:27): "No one knows the Father except the Son and anyone to whom the Son chooses to reveal Him." As this quotation also shows, Jesus also referred to Himself as the Son, a title He uses over and over.

The Holy Spirit is mentioned early in the New Testament (Mt 1:18) when Mary "was found to be with child from the

Holy Spirit." Luke (1:35) more clearly reveals the three Persons of the Trinity through the message of the angel Gabriel to Mary: "The *Holy Spirit* will come upon you, and the power of the *Most High* will overshadow you; therefore the child to be born . . . will be called the *Son* of God" (italics by author).

We learn a great deal about God the Father through His workings in the Old Testament. Jesus reveals Him further in the New Testament as do the inspired writers of the Epistles, particularly John and Paul. At the Last Supper Jesus promises that He will not leave the Apostles orphaned (Jn 14:18) but He will send the Holy Spirit who "will teach you everything, and remind you of all that I have said to you" (Jn 14:26). Just as Matthew begins his Gospel by mentioning the Holy Spirit, so also does he close it (Mt 28:19) when Jesus gives His last and great command: "Go therefore and make disciples of all nations, baptizing them in the name of the Father and of the Son and of the Holy Spirit." Because of this command, the Catholic Church recognizes the baptisms of other Christian churches. However, she does not recognize the baptisms of those (e.g., the Mormons or Jehovah Witnesses) who, while using these words, do not accept the Christian Trinity, three divine Persons in one God. This is a truth that must be accepted through faith in Jesus Christ and not through the use of reason which is incapable of fully understanding it, because it is what the Church calls a mystery.

The catechism *The Teaching of Christ* sums up the Holy Spirit this way:

> The Holy Spirit, a Person distinct from the Father and Son, is equally truly God. In God there is infinite wisdom and infinite love. The Father eternally knows Himself with a perfect Word, an expression of wisdom that fully speaks God's full reality, and this Word is the Son (Jn 1.1,14). The Father and Son love one another with a boundless love, a love that fully expresses all Their reality, a love which is personal and living as are the Father and the Son, and this personal Love proceeding from the Father and the Son is the Holy Spirit. The Spirit is not created; He is a Person co-equal and co-eternal with the Father and the Son.

Thus through the revelation of Jesus Christ, we come to know things about God we could never learn of ourselves. Jesus Christ is both revealing and revealed in Scripture.

Review Questions

Did Jesus claim to be the Messiah? How?
Did Jesus ever claim He was God? Give examples.
What was the key proof of these claims?
Can one deny the resurrection and be a Christian?
How did Jesus reveal the Trinity?

5. The Mission of Jesus

Indeed, I was born guilty, a sinner when my mother conceived me.

Ps 51:5

Thus far we have examined the reality of God, the nature and attributes of God which have been made known through creation and revelation. We have seen how God spoke to us through the prophets who foretold of a promised Messiah who would save God's people. That promised one was Jesus Christ, the Father's final and supreme revelation.

Now we will examine the reasons Jesus came to live among us, His mission, and how that mission was accomplished.

Original Sin. We have seen how God creates out of love but does not force that love on His creation. Angels were put to a test of their free wills and some failed. When God created our first parents, they too were tested and failed. The Catechism tells us (390) that the third chapter of Genesis "affirms a primeval event," a failure of our first parents.

The consequences of that original sin would touch all of succeeding humanity (C 402). St. Paul tells us (Rom 5:12): "Just as sin came into the world through one man, and death came through sin, and so death spread to all because all have sinned. . . ." The death Paul spoke of was not only physical death but also spiritual death. To save humanity from the effects of sin, Jesus Christ came into the world, and Paul found this his consolation: "For just as by the one man's disobedience the many were made sinners, so by the one man's obedience the many will be made righteous" (Rom 5:19). Thus did Paul contrast Adam and Jesus.

Original sin wounded human nature, depriving it of original holiness. As a result of original sin, suffering and death entered the world and are inherited by all of us. Another effect that touches us all is an inclination to evil, called *concupiscence*, which will "persist in man and summon him to spiritual battle" (C 405).

To aid humanity to rise above this fallen human nature, Jesus came into the world, "he is the New Adam, who inaugurates the new creation" (C 504). He is to be an atoning sacrifice for our sins (1 Jn 4:10) and to show us the way to salvation. The Catechism asks the question: "Why Did the Word Become Flesh?" and then answers it with four reasons (457-460).

The Word became flesh for us:

— "in order to save us by reconciling us with God"

— "so that thus we might know God's love"

— "to be our model of holiness"

— "to make us 'partakers of the divine nature' " (cf. 2 Pt 1:4).

Salvation. Early in the Gospel of John (3:1), a Jewish leader comes to Jesus by night to inquire about His teaching. During the course of the conversation Jesus tells Nicodemus (vv. 16-17):

> For God so loved the world that he gave his only Son, so that everyone who believes in him may not perish but may have eternal life.
> Indeed, God did not send the Son into the world to condemn the world, but in order that the world might be saved through him.

The notion of Jesus as Savior is introduced early in Matthew's Gospel (1:21). Before Joseph and Mary lived together, Joseph had a dream in which an angel appeared and told him the child Mary had conceived was by the Holy Spirit, adding, "She will bear a son, and you are to name him Jesus, for he will save his people from their sins." The name Jesus is from the Aramaic *Yesu* which in turn is from the Hebrew *Yehosua* (Joshua) which means "Yahweh is salvation." On the night of Jesus' birth, the angels announced to the shepherds (Lk 2:11): "To you is born this day in the city of David a Savior, who is the Messiah, the Lord." When Jesus approached John the Baptist at the Jordan to be baptized, John declared, "Here is the Lamb of God who takes away the sin of the world" (Jn 1:29).

Salvation is the deliverance of a person from the effects of sin. It is another word for redemption. Only God can give salvation and God's salvation comes to us through the sacrifice of Jesus Christ. As Jesus gave the cup to His Apostles at the Last Supper, He said (Mt 26:27-28): "Drink from it, all of you; for this is my blood of the covenant, which is poured out for many for the forgiveness of sins."

Know God's Love. Of all the biblical writers, the Apostle John saw more clearly than any other the love God has for His human creation. He sums this up in three words that have no equal (1 Jn 4:8): "God is love." In his Gospel and in his Epistles John stresses this theme: God loves us and we should love Him in return. Jesus told Nicodemus (Jn 3:16) that "God so loved the world that he gave his only Son, so that everyone who believes in him . . . may have eternal life."

Love was to be the mark of the Christian because in showing love the Christian was also showing God the Father. At the Last Supper Jesus stressed the necessity of this love and the lengths one should go to show it (Jn 15:12-13): "This is my commandment, that you love one another as I have loved you. No one has greater love than this, to lay down one's life for one's friends." Within hours of saying this Jesus was to prove God's love for us by freely going to a cruel and brutal death on the Cross.

Model of Holiness. Jesus came on earth to show us how we are to live in this world. He is our model of holiness. "Take my yoke upon you, and learn from me," Jesus bade us (Mt 11:29). Jesus told His Apostles (Jn 14:6), "I am the way, and the truth, and the life." Because Jesus is the way, His teachings are direction signs by which we may reach the Father, the supreme Truth. Jesus, however, is more than a mere signpost. He is the model showing us how to live. The faith of a Christian is judged on how close that person mirrors Christ in his or her life. All of us are called to be other Christs.

Partakers in God's Nature. Part of the mission of Jesus was to show that humanity can be made an intimate with God. St. Peter opens his second letter by saying Jesus has given Christians everything necessary for life and holiness so that they can escape the corruption of the world and have a share in the divine nature (2 Pt 1:4). St. Paul tells us (2 Cor 5:17) that by joining our lives to Christ we become a new creation in which everything old has passed away and

everything that remains has become new. Through baptism
the Christian becomes united with Christ in His Mystical
Body and through the Eucharist the union with Christ is real
and substantial. Each of these will be discussed further on.

The mission of Jesus Christ was a mission of
reconciliation between God and humanity. It was not that God
needed to be reconciled to humanity but that humanity
needed to be reconciled to God. Original sin had broken the
creation covenant and a New Covenant was to be made and
sealed in the sacrifice of Jesus Christ. Jesus was to become
the Lamb who takes away the sin of the world and by giving
up His only Son, the Father showed His everlasting love, a
love He desires us to return. Jesus came to redeem us from
sin and the cost of that redemption was His death on Calvary.

Review Questions

How did original sin enter the world?
Why did the Word become flesh?
What does the name "Jesus" mean?
What one word best describes the mission of Jesus?

6. Jesus Founded a Church to Continue His Mission

The public life of Jesus lasted approximately three years. He disappears from the Gospels at the age of twelve. We hear nothing about him again, except that He was a carpenter in Nazareth, until he reemerges at the Jordan River for His baptism by John the Baptist. The first task of Jesus was to assemble an intimate group around him, twelve in number that was reminiscent of the twelve tribes of Israel. They were simply called the Twelve, and later given the name Apostles, from the Greek *apostolos*, meaning "one sent." While Jesus gathered other disciples around Him, the Twelve were the main focus of his attention and instruction. The Twelve were to be the foundation stones for continuing His mission.

The first two Jesus called were Peter and his brother, Andrew, whom He found fishing in the Sea of Galilee. "Follow me," He said, "and I will make you fishers of men" (Mt 4:19). From that time on, Peter was always mentioned as the first and leader of the Apostles. A little further down the lake, He called John and his brother, James, who were also fishermen. These first four Apostles were particularly close to Jesus.

Many think the call of Jesus came to the Apostles out of the blue, but that was not the case. The Gospel of John, whose account of the first call differs somewhat from Matthew's, tells us that the first encounter was at the baptism of Jesus. Andrew and probably John were disciples of the Baptist, who pointed Jesus out to them, calling him "the lamb of God." Andrew and probably John then spent some time with Jesus and were so impressed that Andrew went looking for his brother, Simon, and told him, "We have found the Messiah!" (Jn 1:41). Andrew brought Simon to Jesus who said, "You are to be called Cephas" (which is translated Peter and means Rock).

After training the Twelve, Jesus sent His Apostles to mission among the Jews, telling them (Mt 10:5), "Go nowhere among the Gentiles, and enter no town of the Samaritans, but go rather to the lost sheep of the house of Israel." He did this because the Jews were the people of the Old Covenant and were to be the first invited into the New Covenant. Later He would extend the mission to Samaritans and Gentiles. St. Paul was to follow the same mission method: upon entering a new city, he went first to the synagogue and, upon being rejected, turned to the Gentiles of the city. This early preaching of the Apostles was a call for repentance and preparation for the kingdom that was being born among them.

Jesus knew that His death was not far distant, so He carefully built the foundations of an organization that would carry on His mission. He taught His Apostles by example and precept, reminding them that He had chosen them for the task which lay ahead, not the other way around. He told them that He expected them to get results in bringing others to the kingdom (Jn 15:16). Although He would leave them, Jesus promised that they will not be alone because the Holy Spirit will come to them to guide them. He promised (Jn 14:26):

> "The Advocate, the Holy Spirit, whom the Father will send in my name, will teach you everything, and remind you of all that I have said to you."

What Jesus was doing was laying the foundations of the Church He was forming, a Church that would carry on His teachings and make them known to all people. He selected Peter to be the leader of this new Church, telling him, "You are Peter, and on this rock I will build my church, and the gates of Hades will not prevail against it. I will give you the keys of the kingdom of heaven, and whatever you bind on earth will be bound in heaven, and whatever you loose upon earth will be loosed in heaven" (Mt 76:18-19).

The final instruction before ascending to heaven was that the new Church was to be universal. On the Mount of the Ascension Jesus gave the last order to His Apostles (Mt 28:18-20):

> All authority in heaven and on earth has been given to me. Go therefore and make disciples of all nations, baptizing them in the

name of the Father and of the Son and of the Holy Spirit, and
teaching them to obey everything that I have commanded you.
And remember, I am with you always, until the end of the world.

Mt 28:18-20

It should be noted here that since Jesus promised to be in
His Church until the end of time and that since Peter and the
other Apostles would age and die, Jesus expected them to
appoint successors who would carry on His mission. The
directives and promises Jesus made to His Apostles would
pass on to their successors.

Identifying Marks of Jesus' Church

The Church of Jesus Christ has to be one founded by Him
and not some human agency. To identify this Church Jesus
gave it four marks by which it could be recognized:
— It is ONE, "One Lord, one Faith, one Baptism."
— It is HOLY because of the presence of the Holy Spirit in that
    Church, because its Founder is holy, and because its
    teachings would work towards the sanctification of its
    members.
— It is CATHOLIC, that is universal, open to all people of all
    nations.
— It is APOSTOLIC, tracing its roots back to the Apostles and
    their teaching.

In order to understand these marks, so that the Church of
Jesus can be identified, we will now examine them more
closely.

One (C 813-816). The Church of Jesus Christ is one
because of its source of unity — the Blessed Trinity, one God,
the Father, Son, and Holy Spirit. There is an old saying
identifying the Church of Jesus Christ: "One Lord, one Faith,
one Baptism." Paul told his Christians to "clothe yourselves
with love, which binds everything together in perfect
harmony" (Col 3:14). The prayer of Jesus was for unity in His
Church: "that they may all be one" (Jn 17:21).

Jesus also gave the example of the unity He desires,
likening Himself to a vine: "I am the vine, you are the
branches. Those who abide in me and I in them bear much

fruit, because apart from me you can do nothing" (Jn 15:5). This command of unity was not merely for the Apostles but for all who would follow Christ. Praying over the Apostles for this unity, Jesus said, "I ask not only on behalf of these, but also on behalf of those who will believe in me through their word, that they may all be one" (Jn 17:20).

Holy (C 823-829). The Church of Jesus Christ must be holy because He is present in that Church (Mt 28:20) and He is holy. The Church of Jesus Christ is also holy because Jesus sent the Holy Spirit to be in His Church to make it holy and guard it from error (Jn 15:12-15). The Church of Jesus Christ is to teach holiness to its members (Mt 5:48). Peter reminded the early Christians of this call to holiness, "As he who called you is holy, be holy yourselves in all your conduct; for it is written 'You shall be holy, for I am holy'" (1 Pt 1:15-16). Peter called the apostolic Church "a holy nation, God's own people" (1 Pt 2:9).

Catholic (C 830-835). The Church of Jesus Christ must be catholic (from the Greek *katholikos*, meaning "universal"). God's salvation is meant for all people as He is the creator of all. The last command of Jesus (Mt 28:19) was to take His Church to all nations. The Church of Jesus Christ is catholic because it must strive to bring all peoples under the leadership of God's Son who has universal dominion assigned Him by the Father. From its very beginning the Church had this universal outlook. Referring to preachers of the Gospel, Paul quotes Psalm 19: "'Their voice has gone out to all the earth, and their words to the end of the world'" (Rom 10:18). No command of Christ was more direct or clearly stated than the command to take His Gospel to all peoples.

Apostolic (C 857-865). The Church of Jesus Christ must be able to trace itself to the Apostles who, after the death of Jesus, were to carry forward the teaching given them by the Lord. It is only by going back to the Apostles that a church can trace itself to Jesus Himself. The Church of Jesus Christ has to descend in an unbroken line to the Apostles and be taught today by the direct successor of the Apostles. The Church of Jesus Christ has to teach those doctrines that the Apostles taught and passed on to their successors (2 Tm

1:13-14), not all of which were written down in the Gospels (Jn 21:25); hence the teaching of the Apostles is very important in determining the true Church of Jesus.

Jesus commissioned His Apostles to take to the world the doctrine He had taught them. In case they forgot some teaching, Jesus promised that the Holy Spirit would be sent to "teach you everything and remind you of all that I have said to you" (Jn 14:26). What Jesus taught the Apostles was what God the Father wanted taught: "Whoever does not love me does not keep my words: and the word that you hear is not mine, but is from the Father who sent me" (Jn 14:24). The Father then is sending forth the Apostles to continue the work of the Son and the Apostles in turn are to appoint successors who will carry on the same teaching. Apostolicity is an important mark of the Church of Jesus Christ because it is only to the Apostles and their successors that the promises of Christ hold. Therefore, it is very important to know which is that Church.

Review Questions

How did Jesus begin to organize His Church?
Who were the first four Apostles?
Did they know Jesus before being called?
What Scripture text establishes Peter as head of the Church?
What are the four identifying marks of Jesus' Church?

7. Which Church Did Jesus Establish?

Since Jesus promised that His Church would remain for all time, it has to exist in the world today. But when one looks out at world Christianity, one sees scores and scores of different Christian churches, varying from one another in doctrine and discipline, all sharing in truth to a greater or lesser degree. Yet almost from the very beginning of Christianity (C 817) divisions began to appear, led by people who believed they knew a better way to God. While the original founders may have been guilty of the sin of heresy, apostasy, or schism, as the centuries passed people brought up in these religions adhered to them in good faith. Because they are justified in the faith of baptism (C 818), they bear the name Christian, participating to a greater or lesser degree in the faith established by Jesus Christ. They are people of the Bible, working for their sanctification and seeking to do the will of God as they understand it.

Nevertheless, an impartial observer looking at the Christian world today can only see a scandal of conflicting claims. The "one flock and one shepherd" Jesus counseled does not exist in the hundreds of different churches, each asserting it is the way to God. But since the Church Jesus founded does exist (Mt 28:20), the question arises which one of these Christian churches is that Church? Some will say, "one church is as good as another" or "there are many paths to God." One church is not as good as another, because truth is truth and does not exist in conflicting forms. While there are many paths to God, Jesus, doing the will of the Father, gave the path that the Father wanted people to use to reach Him most directly.

The many churches about which we have been speaking are gathered under three main headings and each will now be described.

Catholic. A world-wide Church whose members are united in the same faith, participate in the same sacraments and are governed under the spiritual leadership of the pope from the See of Peter (Rome). There is in the Catholic Church various modes of celebrating its Liturgy and, while the basic pattern of celebrating the Eucharist and sacraments is the same, there are differences in language, chant, and rubric. These varied forms are referred to as rites and are generically described as Western and Eastern.

Western. The prevailing rite in the West is the Latin or Roman Rite with certain variations: Mozarabic (Toledo), Ambrosian (Milan), Tridentine, and certain adaptations permitted to Dominicans, Carmelites, and Carthusians.

Eastern. While these rites were formerly confined to a geographical area, today emigration has spread their members throughout the world. These Eastern rites are: ALEXANDRIAN (Copts, Ethiopians); ANTIOCHIAN (Maronites, Syrian, Melankarese); ARMENIAN; BYZANTINE (Albanian, Bulgarian, Greek, Byelorussian, Hungarian, Greek Catholic-Melkite, Romanian, Russian, Ruthenian, Slovak, Ukrainian, Serb, Croatian); CHALDEAN (Chaldean, Syro-Malabarese).

Orthodox. "Orthodox" is the collective name of those self-governing churches of Eastern Europe and Asia that gradually separated themselves from Rome between 1054 and 1472. The term "orthodox" is used to differentiate these churches from the Assyrian (Nestorian) and Monophysite churches of the East. Of all the Christian churches, the Orthodox and Catholic are most closely adjoined, sharing in the same sacraments, Eucharist, and priesthood. Except for recognizing the supremacy of the pope, Orthodox have the same faith as Catholics, although clarifications made in more recent years by Catholic councils have not been given assent. The Orthodox follow the Byzantine Liturgy celebrating it in many languages.

Protestant. This also is a collective name for those churches which broke away from the Catholic Church and then from each other. The major Protestant Churches and the sects deriving from them are (see also Chart 1, pp. 56-57): LUTHERANS (Anabaptists, Mennonites, Moravian); CALVINISTS (Unitarian, Presbyterian, Reformed); ANGLICAN (Episcopal,

Methodist [from Methodists: Salvation Army, Methodist Episcopal and a host of African ME churches, Congregational, Pentecostal of many sizes and varieties], Baptists [from Baptists: Disciples of Christ, Assembly of God, Seventh Day Adventists, Church of God], Brethren, Puritans, Quakers, Congregational).

Others. There are other churches which are entirely independent in foundation. MORMON. Although Mormons claim to be Christians, they are not recognized as such because they reject the Christian teaching of the Trinity of one God and three distinct persons. Although they use the word "Trinity," they mean three separate gods, two with physical bodies and the third a spirit. Because of their denial of the Christian Trinity, their baptisms are not held to be valid. The Mormons have had their own divisions: Reorganized Mormons, Temple Lot, Cutlerites, Bickertonites, etc. Mormons were founded early in the nineteenth century by Joseph Smith, a fallen-away Presbyterian, who lived near Rochester, New York.

JEHOVAH'S WITNESSES. Founded in 1884 by Charles Russell from a group of disaffected Adventists. The Witnesses are also not recognized as Christians because they deny the Trinity. There is only one God: Jehovah. Jesus is not a divine person and the Holy Spirit does not exist as a person.

UNIFICATION CHURCH. Again a sect that purports to be Christian but which denies the divinity of Jesus, making Him only "a perfect man," who failed in His mission by failing to find a perfect mate and create a perfect family. The sect came out of the Pentecostal movement.

CHRISTIAN SCIENCE, founded in Boston in 1879 by Mary Baker Eddy, it is a faith healing group with its own doctrinal interpretations.

UNITY came out of Christian Science and took form in 1891 under Charles and Myrtle Fillmore as a faith healing cult. It has elements of Hinduism that teach all will eventually be saved but must pass through various reincarnations until Unity is reached. The cult uses heavy literature promotion that passes from do-goodism to Unity doctrine.

Another heavily promoted sect is the WORLDWIDE CHURCH

Derivation of Protestant Denominations

I f one needs proof for the fallacy of private interpretation of the Bible, this shows what has happened to Christ's prayer of "one flock, one shepherd," and the divisions continue to this day. The chart does not show Eastern Churches or the hundreds of tiny splinter groups in the United States.

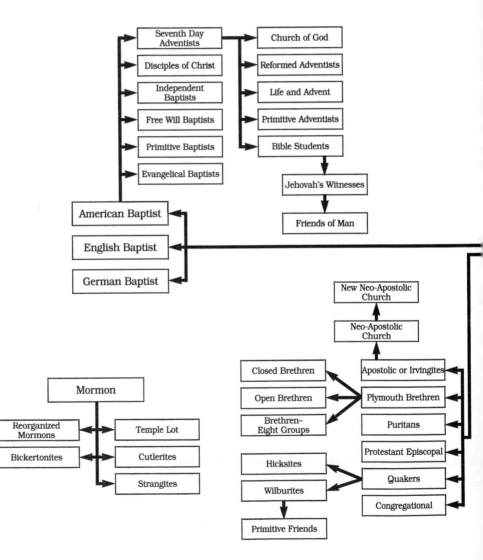

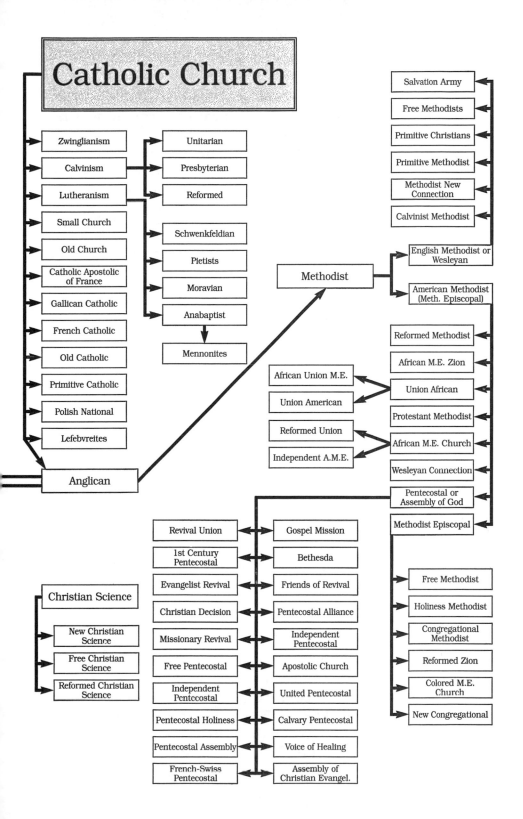

OF GOD, using television, radio, and the printed word. Founded in California by Herbert Armstrong, it promoted a strange amalgam of Judaism and Christianity, denying some essential Christian beliefs. Since the death of Armstrong, the new leaders are bringing it closer to the center.

What is evident in the above listing are the many claims of religious groups to possess the truth. In these days of instant communications through the various media and the home computer, these claims are pressed in multifaceted ways. People of good will and objectivity need a standard by which to judge the many claimants to divine truth. The question these people of good will must ask is "Which is the Church founded by Jesus Christ?" The norms given by Jesus to identify His Church are those mentioned earlier: the Church founded by Jesus Christ is ONE, HOLY, CATHOLIC, and APOSTOLIC.

There are two approaches that can be taken to answer the question, "Which is the true Church of Christ?" One is to proceed negatively and eliminate the claimants one by one until only the true Church remains. The other is positively to make an examination of the one Church which has always made a claim to having the four marks that provide identification. That Church is the Catholic Church.

The Claims of the Catholic Church

At the outset of this investigation, it should be noted that none of these claims can be taken alone. All four of the identification marks given by Jesus must be present at the same time. It is not enough to have two or three of them. If any one of them is lacking, the claim must be denied.

One. The Catholic Church claims to be one and points to its unity in faith, worship, and administration.

Faith. The Catholic Church is one in faith because no matter where in the world one visits, the same faith is being taught. The basic creed for all Catholics is put into a formula that is recited every Sunday by those in attendance at Mass. No matter in what part of the world one lives, no matter the language spoken, the same doctrine is taught. So that the

Time Line of the Churches

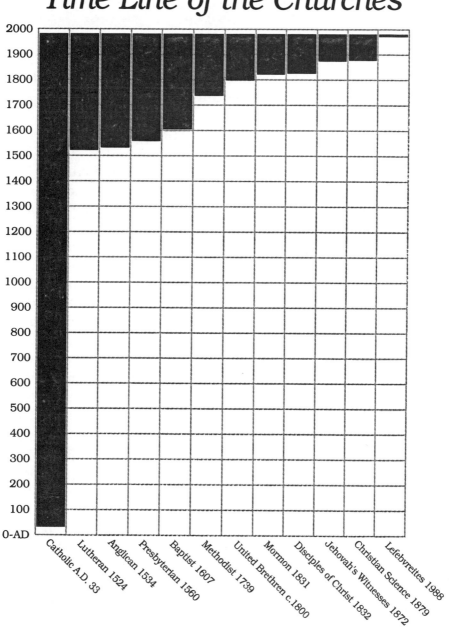

	2000
	1900
	1800
	1700
	1600
	1500
	1400
	1300
	1200
	1100
	1000
	900
	800
	700
	600
	500
	400
	300
	200
	100
	0-AD

Catholic A.D. 33 · Lutheran 1524 · Anglican 1534 · Presbyterian 1560 · Baptist 1607 · Methodist 1739 · United Brethren c.1800 · Mormon 1831 · Disciples of Christ 1832 · Jehovah's Witnesses 1872 · Christian Science 1879 · Lefebvreites 1988

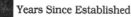 Years Since Established

universal teaching of Catholic faith may be understood, it is made clear to all Catholics in the *Catechism of the Catholic Church*, which was published to guard and present the deposit of faith left to it by the Lord Jesus and taught to it by the Apostles.

Unity applies to belief and worship and does not rule out diversity. Catholics speak a diversity of languages and represent a diversity of nations. The Church is composed of peoples of various cultures. Within the Church there are a diversity of roles — "different gifts, offices, conditions, and ways of life" (C 814). All of these different roles come together in one, universal bond of charity.

Worship. Throughout the Church there is the same celebration of divine worship (C 815), especially through the Sacrifice of the Mass and the celebration of the sacraments. The central act of public worship to which all Catholics are bound each Sunday and holy day is the Mass. There are differences in this worship according to the solemnity of the occasion, the language, or rite used. The prophet Malachi (1:11) has God asking for a worship that will exist "from the rising of the sun to its setting my name is great among the nations, and in every place incense is offered to my name. . . ." No matter the hour, day or night, the Sacrifice of the Mass is being offered to God somewhere in the world. It should also be noted that, outside Catholic and Orthodox liturgies, no where else is sacrificial offering made to God, not in Protestantism, nor Islam, nor Judaism.

Administration. In the Catholic Church there is a unity in administration or government. The head of the Church is Jesus Christ, who acts through His vicar on earth, the pope, who is the successor of St. Peter. Acting with the pope are the bishops, the successors of the Apostles, who with the pope make up the Magisterium, or teaching authority of the Church. Assisting the bishops are pastors or priests, who along with the hierarchy are shepherds of the people of God. Thus there is a vertical unity and a horizontal unity with people united to one another in the Mystical Body of Christ (Jn 15:5).

Holy. The Catholic Church claims holiness because of the presence in it of its founder, Jesus Christ (Mt 28:20) and the presence of the Holy Spirit (Jn 16:13). The teachings of the Catholic Church have come to it from Jesus Christ through the Apostles. It places before its members and the world the highest standards of perfection. Many of its members are in religious communities with vows of perpetual poverty, chastity, and obedience. The Church is recognized by the world as a moral bulwark against divorce, birth prevention, abortion, oppression of workers, and many other civil evils.

The holiness of the Church is reflected in lives of heroic sanctity of many of its members, proven by miracles, and given the title of Saint (Holy One) as an inspiration and model for all Catholics. Through the example of these saints, Catholics are urged beyond the minimum necessary for salvation and are urged to seek spiritual perfection. Not all Catholics accept this spiritual challenge, for there are failures, just as there were failures among Christ's disciples (Jn 6:66, Mt 26:14, Mt 26:75). Nevertheless, the Church continually calls upon its members to seek higher spiritual perfection.

The holiness of the Catholic Church is exemplified in its spiritual life, particularly through the administration of its seven sacraments which are means established by Christ to give grace at a particular time in life, and mainly through the Eucharist which is the abiding presence of Jesus in His Church.

Catholic (Universal). Jesus told his Apostles that they were to take the new religion into the whole world (Mt 28:19) and, since that command, the Catholic Church has been concerned with the evangelization of people of every nation and race. Over the centuries, thousands upon thousands of Catholic men and women have labored to make the faith of Jesus Christ known, often at the cost of their own lives. Catholicism is not the property of any race or color or nation. It is not a Church of England, or a Greek or Russian Orthodox Church. It is as its name implies, a universal Church.

Apostolic. Of all the marks of the Church, that of apostolic differentiates it from all Protestant churches. Both the Catholic and Orthodox churches can establish apostolic origins, with the Orthodox making a final break with the See of Peter in the fifteenth century, although in recent years some rapprochement is being made. All of the Protestant churches originated in human founders — Martin Luther, John Calvin, Henry VIII, John Knox, the Wesley brothers, Alexander Campbell, and so on. Breakaway churches are still being founded today.

It is an established historical fact that the Catholic Church can trace itself back through pope after pope to the first pope, St. Peter, who was put in charge by Christ Himself (Mt 16:18-19). Likewise, the bishops of the Catholic Church are descended in line from the Apostles. While the early Church was an underground Church, assailed and persecuted, it emerged with the peace of Constantine who built the first basilica to honor St. Peter over the Apostle's burial place and gave to the pope the basilica of St. John Lateran, founded 1200 years before the emergence of Protestantism and which is still the pope's official see-church.

Since Jesus promised to be with His Church for *all* time, it follows that His apostolic Church exists today. It is only the Catholic Church that can cite a direct historical succession to establish its apostolicity. Other churches may claim it but it is only the Catholic Church which holds a clear title — its unbroken list of successive popes.

Can Protestants Be Saved?

St. Cyprian stated the necessity for belonging to the Church Jesus established: "Outside the Church, there is no salvation." Vatican Council II in its Dogmatic Constitution on the Church (no. 14) restated this principle: "Basing itself on scripture and tradition, it [this holy Council] teaches that the Church, a pilgrim now on earth, is necessary for salvation: the one Christ is mediator and the way of salvation; he is present to us in his body which is the Church. He himself explicitly asserted the necessity of faith and baptism (cf. Mk. 16:16; Jn. 3:5), and thereby affirmed at the same time the necessity of the Church which men enter through baptism as through a door. Hence they could not be saved who, knowing that the Catholic Church was founded as necessary by God through Christ, would refuse either to enter it, or remain in it."

Consider that last sentence in the above quotation carefully. What it means is that salvation would be denied to anyone who *knew* the Catholic Church was the true Church and for one reason or another refused to join it. It does not mean that a sincere and honest Protestant (or Jew or Muslim) belonging to his or her religious community in good faith would be lost. God's condemnation is reserved for deliberate and grave faults, not for one who seeks to serve God according to his or her conscience.

Therefore, a baptized Protestant who has no doubt in his or her church can find salvation. In desiring to do God's will, the non-Catholic Christian would enter the Catholic Church if he or she knew that was where God's grace was leading. As it is, the baptized Protestant is united to Jesus through baptism. Sacred Scripture is held in honor as a rule of faith and life. Many Protestants have shed their blood for their beliefs and are honored as martyrs. At the same time we should not forget the prayer of Jesus for unity, and our own prayer should be for the day when all Christians will once again be one and the scandal of a divided Christianity is no more.

Since non-Catholic Christians can find salvation, there are those who say no approaches should be made to bring them into the Catholic Church. They use the word "proselytize" as if it was some evil and despicable thing. Yet the prayer of Jesus is for the unity of Christianity (Jn 17:20-21) and that all be united in one faith with Him and that all may be joined in the fullness of truth that Jesus and the Apostles taught. To be completely honest with God, the question — "Which is the Church Jesus founded?" — is one each person of good will should strive to answer.

Review Questions

What are the three major Christian divisions?
How is the Catholic Church divided?
What is the basic difference between Catholics and Orthodox?

Why are such sects as Mormons and Jehovah's Witnesses not
considered Christian?
How can the true Church be identified?
How does the Catholic Church meet this test?
Can those outside the true Church be saved?
If someone asked which is the Church Jesus founded, how
would you prove your answer?

The Catholic Church Is a Biblical Church (C 101-133)

Most Protestants consider themselves people of the Book.
Indeed, "*Sola Scriptura*" (Scripture Alone), was the rallying cry
of the Reformation. Protestants proclaim that Scripture is the
sole source of belief and that each reader of Scripture may
privately and accurately interpret what he or she reads
therein.

The accusation is made by many that Catholics are
forbidden to read the Bible, that Catholic doctrine is
man-made, and that "the Catholic Church even chained the
Bible so that people couldn't take it and read it." Perhaps in
the past there were chained Bibles, but until John Gutenberg
invented moveable type (c. 1440), Bibles were copied by hand
and a complete Bible was very precious and was protected
and guarded. With the invention of mechanical printing,
Bibles could be printed in quantities. The Anglican King
James Bible in English was published in 1611. Catholics,
however, published an English translation of the New
Testament in 1582 and the Old Testament in 1609; combined
they were known as the Douay Version of the Holy Bible.

With printed Bibles Catholics were encouraged to have a
Bible in their homes and were given incentives for regular
reading of the Bible. What they were not encouraged to do
was to interpret it for themselves, as were Protestants, but to
depend upon the Church for the correct interpretation. The
Catholic Church teaches that Sacred Scripture must be
interpreted "in the light of the same Spirit by whom it was
written." But this determination of what the Spirit inspired
cannot be left to private interpretation. Two persons reading

the same passage can come to opposite opinions, and both cannot be correct. In fact, as history shows, Protestantism has resulted in a whole plethora of churches and sects because of private interpretation.

The Catholic Church reserves final interpretation to itself because of its belief in the promise of Jesus to be in the Church for all time and His promise to send the Holy Spirit to guide the Church in truth: "When the Spirit of truth comes, he will guide you into all the truth" (Jn 16:13). Because the Spirit is truth and the Spirit is in the Church, when the Church acts in conjunction with the Spirit, truth results.

Since the Bible is truth and inspired by the Spirit, nothing the Catholic Church teaches can contradict the Bible. That is why in the preparation of this book, scriptural references are made so frequently. Catholic devotions are founded in Scripture. The Mass from its beginning to end is rooted in Scripture. The Rosary, a popular Catholic devotion in honor of the Virgin Mary, is made up of scriptural prayer: the Our Father given us by Jesus, the Hail Mary built on the greetings of the Angel Gabriel and that of Elizabeth when Mary visited her. The Breviary which each priest recites daily is made up of psalms, scriptural readings, and prayers taken directly from Scripture.

Tradition

The Church has always claimed two sources of Divine Revelation: Sacred Scripture and Sacred Tradition. The "Scripture alone" of the Protestant Reformers discarded Tradition; this was a serious mistake because it cut them off from apostolic teaching.

At the outset of a consideration of Tradition, a distinction has to be made between *Tradition* and *tradition,* since both words are used in the Church. Tradition with a capital T refers to Apostolic Tradition. This Tradition "comes from the apostles and hands on what they received from Jesus' teaching and example and what they learned from the Holy Spirit" (C 83). Tradition with a small t refers to the "various theological, disciplinary, liturgical, or devotional traditions, born in the local churches over time. As the Catechism tells us, "In the light of Tradition, these traditions can be retained, modified or even abandoned under the guidance of the Church's magisterium" (C 83). Tradition with a small t is nothing more than time-honored custom and usage, and can be changed. Tradition with a capital T and Sacred Scripture make up a single sacred deposit of the Word of God.

It must be remembered that the New Testament did not exist in the early Church. The teaching of Jesus was passed on orally by the Apostles and those who knew Jesus. Thus was oral Tradition born. From this oral Tradition the Gospels were formed. The Gospel of Luke is a Gospel of Tradition since he did not know Jesus. Mark wrote down what Peter had told him. If we accept the Gospel of John as a product of his old age, then he was only writing down stories, events, and teachings that he had long been telling orally. Indeed at the end of his Gospel, John sums up: "This is the disciple who is bearing witness to these things, and who has written these things; and we know that his testimony is true. But there are also many other things that Jesus did; were every one of them to be written, I suppose that the world itself could not contain the books that would be written."

The importance of Apostolic Tradition was held in great honor by the early Church. St. Paul was very clear in his appreciation of Apostolic Tradition. He told his disciple Timothy, who had become a bishop (2 Tm 2:2): "What you have heard from me through many witnesses entrust to faithful people who will be able to teach others as well." Paul warned against those who were not living according to the Tradition he had passed on (2 Thes 3:6). Although Paul made known Tradition through his Epistles, he also did it by word of mouth (2 Thes 2:15). All of the Epistles concern the setting down of Apostolic Tradition, but a great deal more was given orally. For this we have to depend on the Fathers of the Church, particularly Christian leaders who knew the Apostles and in turn passed on what they had learned. Books such as the *Didache* (Teaching of the Twelve Apostles) take on great importance. Today too little attention is paid to the teaching of the Church Fathers and the theological science of patristics is too little appreciated. It was the Fathers, guided by the Holy Spirit, who selected the works that we now call Sacred Scripture. It was the Fathers who composed the statement of basic beliefs that we know as the Apostles' Creed. It was the Fathers who developed the form of Catholic worship that we now call the Liturgy. It was the Fathers on the basis of the teaching of the Apostles who condemned heresies and began the sacred science we know as theology. It was the Fathers who gave ordered form to the Church. All of this is part of Apostolic Tradition that so many Christians now reject.

The Church Fathers of Vatican Council II in their Dogmatic Constitution on Divine Revelation (nos. 9, 10) spoke of the close relationship between Scripture and Tradition: "Sacred Tradition and sacred Scripture, then, are bound closely together, and communicate one with the other. For both of them, flowing out from the same divine well-spring, come together in some fashion to form one thing, and move towards the same goal. Sacred Scripture is the speech of God as it is put down in writing under the breath of the Holy Spirit. And Tradition transmits in its entirety the Word of God which has been entrusted to the apostles by Christ the Lord and the Holy Spirit. It transmits it to the successors of the apostles so that, enlightened by the Spirit of truth, they may faithfully preserve, expound and spread it abroad by their preaching. Thus it comes about that the Church does not draw her certainty about all revealed truths from the holy Scriptures alone. Hence, both Scripture and Tradition must be accepted and honored with equal feelings of devotion and reverence."

The Magisterium

At this point it would be well to speak of the Magisterium of the Church. The Magisterium is the teaching authority of the Catholic Church (from Latin *magister*, meaning teacher). It is composed of the pope (the successor to Peter) and the bishops (successors to the Apostles). We know from Scripture (1 Tm 3:1-5) that bishops were part of the governance of the Apostolic Church. The teaching of the Apostles formed the deposit of faith which was to be entrusted to their successors who were to teach it correctly and without change. Thus Paul would instruct Timothy (2 Tm 1:13-14): "Hold to the standard of sound teaching that you have heard from me. . . . Guard the good treasure entrusted to you, with the help of the Holy Spirit. . . ."

The original Magisterium of the Church was Christ; then His appointees, Peter and the Apostles, and finally the successor of Peter and the successors of the Apostles. The Catechism (890) tells us that "The mission of the Magisterium is linked to the definitive nature of the covenant established by God with his people in Christ." The Magisterium is the authentic teacher of the apostolic faith, endowed under the authority of Christ, who commanded (Mt 28:20) Peter and the Apostles to teach all peoples "everything that I have commanded you. And remember, I am with you always, to the end of the age."

"It is this Magisterium's task to preserve God's people from deviations and defections and to guarantee them the objective possibility of professing the true faith without error" (C 890). Although the Church has theologians and philosophers, they are not part of the Magisterium, which is limited to pope and bishops, as Pope John Paul II affirmed in *Dei Verbum* (no. 10): "the task of authentically interpreting the word of God, whether in its written form or that of Tradition, has been entrusted only to those charged with the Church's living Magisterium, whose authority is exercised in the name of Jesus."

The teaching of the Magisterium is the guide for the Catholic conscience. As Vatican Council II taught, "In forming their consciences the faithful must pay careful attention to the sacred and certain teaching of the Church. For the Catholic Church is by the will of Christ the teacher of truth. It is her duty to proclaim and teach with authority the truth which is Christ and, at the same time, to declare and confirm by her authority the principles of the moral order which spring from human nature itself" (On Religious Liberty, 14). The Magisterium's duty is to remind the Christian conscience of truths it should already possess for as John Paul II points out, "Freedom of conscience is never freedom 'from' truth but always and only freedom 'in' truth" (The Splendor of Truth, 64).

While most Protestants believe in the private interpretation of Scripture, in the Catholic Church the final interpreter of Scripture is its Magisterium. It was the early Magisterium of the Church that gave us the Bible. It was the Fathers who assembled seventy-two individual books and formed them into one canon. It was the Magisterium that interpreted these books. This system lasted for fifteen hundred years until some reformers decided to toss out some books and leave the Bible open to everyone's private interpretation. Unfortunately with this latter system, the Holy Spirit is removed because the Holy Spirit cannot be self-contradictory.

In some places it is argued today that the Magisterium violates the freedom of conscience and some theologians speak of "the authority of conscience." Conscience, however, has to conform to God's moral law, otherwise it is a false conscience. Conscience has to judge truth as revealed by God and in the person of Jesus Christ. There is no right to do wrong and there is no right to believe error. It is the duty of the Magisterium to reveal that truth which really makes one free (Jn 8:32). Morality is not decided by a majority opinion of private interpreters.

Infallibility

Perhaps no claim of the Catholic Church is as controverted by those outside it than is its claim of infallibility. As the Catechism (C 889) puts it, "In order to preserve the Church in the purity of the faith handed on by the apostles, Christ who is the Truth willed to confer on her a share in his own infallibility." It is the task of the Magisterium to keep people from doctrinal error and to guarantee them the objective possibility of professing the true faith without error. This infallibility exists in:

— the pope
— the body of bishops acting in unity with the pope
    This infallibility pertains only to:

— matters concerning faith and morals
— divine revelation (Sacred Scripture)

Infallibility does not mean impeccability, that is, the inability to fall into sin. Peter thrice denied the Lord and there have been popes whose personal lives were not exemplary. Each pope and bishop must work out his own salvation as does every other Christian. Infallibility does not mean that the pope is inspired or subject to a sudden revelation; he is only proclaiming as correct what is already there. He is not infallible when he speaks on science or sports or any topic that has no connection with religion. The pope or pope and bishops are infallible only when they speak on matters already in the deposit of faith (Scripture or Tradition). Divine revelation ended with the Apostles and there are no new revelations to be made.

Infallibility also does not exist in the person but in the office that person holds. In the case of the pope, he does not make an infallible pronouncement as a private person but solely as the successor of Peter, and the bishops as successors to the Apostles.

The Necessity of Infallibility

It has already been shown that Jesus established a Church that was to last for all time and that He would be constantly with the Church (Mt 28:20). He also promised the leaders of that Church that he would send them the Holy Spirit as a guide and that the Spirit would be sent "to be with you forever" (Jn 14:16). He also gave assurance that Satan would not prevail against the Church (Mt 16:18). The purpose of this divine Presence in the Church is to guard it from error and to keep it secure in the teachings of Jesus until the end of time. This can only be done by giving the Church infallibility in those teachings.

Jesus also made clear that this infallibility applied in a particular way to the office of Peter. At the end of the Gospel of John (21:15-17) the risen Jesus takes Peter aside and in a parallel to Peter's three denials of Jesus, the Lord asks Peter three times, "Do you love me?" Three times Peter replies in the affirmative, and each time Jesus tells Peter to feed and tend His sheep. The head of the new Church was to feed the faithful with correct doctrine and, in order to do that, Jesus would have to protect Peter and his successors from error. Infallibility in doctrine then becomes a necessity.

The necessity of infallibility becomes even more clear when we consider Sacred Scripture. All Christians agree on the infallibility of the Bible. But if everyone is free to decide what the Bible means, no one can be sure what it means. God gave us the Bible to reveal Himself and show us His way for us to live. He meant it to be correctly understood in accordance with the inspiration He gave the writer. However, for it to be correctly understood, an infallible interpreter is needed, for an infallible Bible without an infallible interpreter is a meaningless Bible.

If lies and error could enter the Church's teaching, Christ's promise in Matthew 16:18 could not be true because Satan the father of lies would be in the Church. If error could enter the Church's teaching, then the Church would not be "the pillar and bulwark of the truth" that Paul declared it to be (1 Tm 3:15). All of this can be put in syllogistic form: "The Holy Spirit is an infallible teacher. The Holy Spirit guides the teaching of the Church of Christ. Therefore the Church of Christ is infallible in its teaching." The major and minor premises have already been proven, hence the conclusion is inescapable.

Review Questions

Prove that the Catholic Church is a biblical church.
Why is private interpretation of the Bible wrong?
If we cannot interpret the Bible for ourselves, how do we know what it means?
What are the two sources of Catholic belief?
What is the difference between Sacred Tradition and tradition?
What is the Magisterium? Of whom is it composed?
What is the role of the Magisterium?
What is infallibility? To what does it pertain?
Who is infallible?
Why is infallibility necessary?

The Catholic Church Is a Hierarchical Church

God is the ruler of the universe. He is so by right of creation. God shares His dominion over the earth with human leaders. God is not concerned with who Caesar is but with what Caesar does. Americans are brought up to believe that democracy is the best form of government and in their parroting of "one person, one vote," one would think that Utopia had arrived. There are those who believe that the Church should be democratic, "one person, one vote," that Church leaders should be elected by popular vote, and that Church doctrine should be decided by majority vote.

But God is not a democrat. He is the creator who lays down the rules for human conduct in His commandments which are made known to us through His inspired Sacred Scripture. He doesn't ask us to vote on what we should do; He tells us. But as pointed out early in this book, God is love who wants only good for His human creation. When through original sin, human integrity was lost, God the Father did not forget His human creation but promised a Savior and Redeemer. In the course of time the divine Son of the Father was born, Jesus Christ, whose stay on earth was but to be for a brief time. In preparation for His departure, Jesus selected twelve men and appointed one of them, Simon Peter, as leader, and established them as governors and teachers of the Church that would carry on His mission. The Church Jesus founded was not a democratic one but a hierarchical Church where authority came down from God the Father, through the Son, to the supreme bishop (Peter and his successors), who in turn was assisted by his fellow Apostles (bishops and their successors). The hierarchy that was established was to be a teaching hierarchy, a collegial hierarchy, a sacramental hierarchy, and a hierarchy of service. Pope and bishops form what is known as the episcopal college (C 880) or permanent assembly, at the head of which is the successor of Peter, the Roman Pontiff.

The Pope

The Pope, Supreme Pontiff of the Universal Church, Patriarch of the West, Bishop of Rome, Vicar of Christ, Servant of the Servants of God, is pastor of the entire Church. He has full, supreme, universal power over the whole Church, a power he can always exercise unhindered. The pope's task is to be governor, sanctifier, and caretaker of the Church on earth, of which Jesus Christ is the true head. The pope has unusual power, for in giving Peter the keys of heaven, Jesus also gave assurance that what the pope bound on earth would be recognized in heaven.

Because of these claims, nowhere else does anti-Catholic sentiment center as it does in the papacy, because if the claims were admitted as true the whole underpinnings of non-Catholic churches would collapse. The pope is vilified, called the beast of Revelation, a tool of Satan, the anti-Christ, and almost every ugly name that can be imagined. When cartoonists wish to attack the Church, it is usually through a caricature of the pope attached to some Catholic doctrine. Even today when anti-Catholicism tries to be subtle, certain publishers make a living by pope bashing.

Other less virulent critics argue that the claims about the papacy mentioned above were not present in the early Church. It may be that they were not there full blown but they were present in embryo. The Church is a living organism and like all living organisms is subject to growth and development. The history of the early Church shows this development. Pope St. Clement, a successor of Peter and in whose Roman home Peter is believed to have resided, censured Corinthian Christians and ruled on the succession of bishops, his letter indicating the authority of the pope beyond Rome. St. Ignatius of Antioch on his way to martyrdom in Rome wrote ahead to the pope; St. Polycarp went to Rome to settle the date for Easter.

St. Cyprian of Carthage wrote from North Africa: "It is on him (Peter) that He (Jesus) builds the Church, and to him that He entrusts to feed His sheep. Although He gave power to all the Apostles, yet He founded a single chair, thus establishing by His authority the font and benchmark of the Churches' oneness. If a man does not hold fast to this oneness of Peter, does he imagine that he still holds the faith? If he deserts the Chair of Peter upon whom the Church was built, does he believe he is in the same Church?"

St. Ambrose (c. 380) summed up all that had gone on before: "*Ubi Petrus, ibi Ecclesia*" — "Where Peter is, there is the Church."

The College of Bishops

The college of bishops (C 886) is made up of "individual *bishops* [who] are the visible source and foundation of unity in their own particular Churches (dioceses)." In their dioceses they partake in the pope's teaching, sanctifying, and governing offices. As a body they have no authority unless united with Peter's successor. When they come together with the pope in synod or council, they have full and supreme authority over the universal Church.

Each bishop in his diocese is assisted by priests and deacons who together compose the clergy and staff the various parishes and diocesan offices. Bishops are appointed by the pope and must be ordained by other valid bishops to continue the apostolic succession. Although each bishop is given care of a territory and is expected to exercise his vocation as pastor, teacher, and governor, all are expected (C 886) to contribute also "to the welfare of the whole Mystical Body," (*Lumen Gentium*, 23) that is to the entire Church, particularly where there are needs.

The Commandments of the Church

The basic law of the Catholic Church, as it is of all Christian churches, resides in the Ten Commandments given to Moses and passed down through the people of Israel. In addition, the Church has the six precepts of its own which all Catholics are expected to observe. These are:

1. *"You shall attend Mass on Sundays and holy days of obligation."* Sundays are a yearlong celebration of Easter and

all Catholics are obliged to gather for the Eucharistic celebration commemorating the resurrection of the Lord.

2. *"You shall confess your sins at least once a year."* This precept "ensures preparation for the Eucharist by the reception of the sacrament of reconciliation (penance), which continues baptism's work of conversion and forgiveness" (C 2042).

3. *"You shall receive your Creator in Holy Communion at least during the Easter season."* While Catholics are encouraged in frequent reception of the Eucharist, ideally each time they take part in the Eucharistic celebration, this law ensures annual reception of the Lord's Body and Blood, particularly in connection with the Paschal celebration.

4. *"You shall keep holy the holy days of obligation."* This commandment completes the Sunday observation by requiring presence at certain feasts of the Lord, the Virgin Mary, and the saints. There are variations of this precept in different parts of the world.

5. *"You shall observe the prescribed days of fast and abstinence."* Penance and sacrifice are important preparation for liturgical feasts as well as ways to acquire mastery over ourselves.

6. *"You have the obligation of providing for the material needs of the Church, according to your abilities."*

The Law of the Church

"Since the Church is organized as a social and visible structure," Pope John Paul II wrote in issuing a revised Code of Canon Law following Vatican Council II, "it must have norms: in order that its hierarchical and organic structure be visible; in order that the functions divinely entrusted to it, especially that of sacred power and of the administration of the sacraments, may be adequately organized; in order that the mutual relations of the faithful may be regulated according to justice based upon charity, with the rights of individuals guaranteed and well defined; in order, finally, that common initiatives undertaken to live a Christian life ever more perfectly may be sustained, strengthened and fostered by canonical norms."

This body of law which governs Catholic life consists of 1,752 canons, divided into seven books: 1. General Norms, 2. The People of God, 3. The Teaching Office of the Church, 4. The Office of Sanctifying in the Church; 5. The Temporal Goods of the Church, 6. Sanctions in the Church, 7. Processes. There is a commission set up at the Vatican that rules on the correct interpretation of the canons, whenever a doubt is raised.

Canon law is as old as the Church. In the Book of Acts we read of laws being enacted. Problems raised by St. Paul concerning his gentile converts were settled in what is called the Council of Jerusalem (Acts 15). The writings of St. Paul give many examples of laws governing Christian life. The law given by St. Paul (1 Cor 7:12-15) on his apostolic authority governing a convert whose pagan spouse refuses to continue married life is still in effect in canon law 1143.

Following the apostolic era, the Edict of Constantine allowed the Church to emerge from the catacombs and more formal organization took place. The first of the ecumenical councils, the Council of Nicaea, was held in AD 325 and produced the Creed of Christian belief which is still recited in the Sunday Liturgy. This council also passed regulations of pastoral practice and Church discipline. The pope and councils ever since then have continued to enact legislation to govern the Church and its faithful people.

Church law exists, Pope John Paul II writes, so that "the salvation of souls may be rendered ever more easy."

The Missionary Nature of the Church

The very first canon law (204) dealing with the people of God states:

> The Christian faithful are those who, inasmuch as they have been incorporated in Christ through baptism, have been constituted as the people of God; for this reason . . . they are called to exercise

Doctrinal Comparison

Apostolic Teaching	Catholicism	Protestantism
Eucharist		
True Body and Blood of Christ under the appearance of bread and wine	True Body and Blood of Christ under the appearance of bread and wine	Christ present only as symbol*
Penance		
Christ gave Apostles and successors power to forgive and retain sins	Christ gave Apostles and successors power to forgive and retain sins	Rejection of Catholic claim
Marriage		
Valid marriage indissoluble	Valid marriage indissoluble	Divorce permitted
Biblical Interpretation		
Interpreted by Church	Interpreted by Church	Private Interpretation
Papacy		
Christ chose Peter and meant for him to have successors	Pope successor of Peter	Catholic claim denied
Infallibility		
Christ grants to Church	Pope and bishops infallible	Catholic claim denied
Abortion		
"Do not kill a fetus by abortion or commit infanticide" *(Didache)*	Absolutely forbidden	Generally allowed by main line churches, some exceptions
Tradition		
Cited as rule by Apostles	Source of faith with Scripture	Generally denied

* *Some Anglicans (Episcopals) hold Catholic position (transubstantiation); Lutherans approach Catholic teaching (transignification).*

For explanation of Apostolic and Catholic positions, consult text.

the mission which God has entrusted to the Church to fulfill in the world, in accord with the condition proper to each one.

The "mission which God has entrusted to the Church" is summarized in the Great Command Jesus gave to take His Gospel to all peoples, baptizing them and teaching them to obey all that He commanded (Mt 28:19-20). The Church, then, is missionary by its very nature and each Catholic has the duty to spread the Gospel. Canon 211 states:

All the Christian faithful have the duty and the right to work so that the divine message of salvation may increasingly reach the whole of humankind in every age and in every land.

Paul's agonized cry (1 Cor 9:16), "Woe to me if I do not proclaim the Gospel!", indicates the depths of the missionary mandate placed on the Church, the ultimate purpose of which "is none other than to make men share in the communion between the Father and Son in their spirit of love" (C 850). Love by its very nature is diffusive, and as Paul says (2 Cor 5:14) "the love of Christ urges us on." It is because of God's universal plan of salvation that the Church must be missionary. Missionary effort also is concerned with that unity for which Jesus prayed, even if that effort is directed toward others joined by baptism, but "yet separated from full communion with her" (C 855).

Ecumenism. Despite Christ's desire for unity in His Church (Jn 17:21), there are many who believe the Church should not reach out to those who, while joined by baptism, are not yet joined in faith. The reasoning goes that since other Christians can achieve salvation on their own (Dogmatic Constitution on the Church, 15), they should not be disturbed in conscience, and the Church should not make enemies by attempted recruitment. The fallacy in this approach is that it negates Christ's hope of "one flock, one shepherd." If Catholics truly believe that their Church is the Church Christ founded and to which He wishes all to belong, then they should not be hesitant to promote inquiry into that Church by respectful and fraternal approaches to others of good will.

Unity is what ecumenism is all about. Of what then does the ecumenical movement consist? First, on the part of Catholics there should be a genuine desire to understand the faith of our separated brethren. For too long the various Christian communities have been separated without dialogue or an understanding of each other. By revealing ourselves to each other, we often find that there is more on which we agree than what separates us. Misunderstandings built up and magnified over the centuries are dissipated in mutual respect. Dialogue can be carried on among religious leaders and among Christians themselves.

There are many areas of social service in which Catholics and other Christians can collaborate, in our communities, nation, and the world. The Decree on Ecumenism (no. 12) makes a point of calling for this type of unified action, particularly in regions where social and technological evolution are taking place. Ecumenism should use every possible means to relieve the afflictions of our times, such as famine and natural disasters, illiteracy and poverty, lack of housing and the unequal distribution of wealth. "Through such cooperation, all believers in Christ are able to learn easily how they can understand each other better and esteem each other more, and how the road to unity can be made smooth."

Finally, there should be ecumenical prayer. The decree calls public and private prayer for the unity of Christians the soul of the whole ecumenical movement. Faith and unity are a gift of the Spirit and prayers for unity by those separated by doctrine and practice ensures the presence of Christ among them, "For where two or three are gathered in my name, I am there among them" (Mt 18:20). And with Christ all things are possible.

Review Questions

What is the hierarchy? Who composes it?
Is the Catholic Church democratic? Explain your answer.
Give some of the titles of the pope.
Why is the papacy so often attacked?
How did St. Ambrose summarize his teaching on the Church?

What is the College of Bishops? Who is its head?
What are the six commandments of the Church?
Why is canon law necessary?
What is the desired end of ecumenism?
Discuss ecumenism true and false.

8. The Church Is Hierarchical

Jesus is the founder of the Church and its source of ministry (C 874). His teachings were to be carried to all the world, its people initiated into the Church through baptism, and the teachings of Jesus passed on to them (Mt 28:19-20). Those who entered the Church were to be fed the truths of God and shepherded along the path of eternal salvation (Jn 21:17). In order to accomplish this, Jesus formed an apostolic band of twelve Apostles (Lk 6:13) whom He trained and sent out on missions (Mk 6:7). He selected Simon Peter to be the head of this band (Mt 16:18-19) and since the Church was to endure for all time, that band was to appoint successors (Acts 1:26). These successors were known as bishops who in turn were assisted by ordained ministers (Phil 1:1 and 1 Tm 4:14). As the numbers in the Church grew, a variety of offices were established to serve the people of God (Acts 6:3-4).

As with any living organism, there was growth and expansion. The Church developed, accordingly as needs arose, but always on the foundation Christ had ordained. The Catholic Church we see in the world today is a result of that growth, a Church always faithful to its apostolic origins, but adaptable to or protective against changing times. Over the centuries at irregular intervals ecumenical (Greek, *ecumenos*, of the whole world) councils have been held which bring together all the bishops of the world under the leadership and authority of the pope, the results of which are binding on the Catholic conscience. In more recent years there was the Council of Trent (1545-1563) to consider problems caused by the Protestant Reformation, Vatican Council I (1869-1870) to consider the nature of the Church in the face of such new heresies as Modernism, and Vatican Council II (1962-1965) to restate doctrine in the contemporary and changing technological world. Vatican II was the twenty-first such council since the foundation of the Church.

We will now consider the various grades within the hierarchy that is charged with governance and spiritual concern for the people of God.

The Papacy

No office within the Catholic Church disturbs some people as much as that of the pope. It is on the papacy that anti-Catholic bias seems to concentrate. Since the earliest days of the United States the pope has been lampooned, defamed, burned in effigy, vilely caricatured by cartoonists, labeled the Anti-Christ and Revelation's beast of the Apocalypse. In the days of the Know-Nothings, while they practiced violence against foreign-born Catholics, particularly Irish, burned schools and convents, and inflicted personal injury, their Catholic hatred was focused on the pope. Thomas Nast, noted for his cartoons against Tammany Hall, was also celebrated for his cartoons attacking pope and bishops. When the Washington Monument was being built, foreign governments were asked to contribute a stone for its construction. The pope, who at the time was both spiritual ruler of the Church and temporal ruler of the Papal States, sent a stone but Know-Nothings threw it into the Potomac River and it was never recovered. While anti-Catholicism is more subtle today, there are still people who make a living by papal bashing.

This hatred of the papacy, while not reasonable, is understandable. To admit the claims of the papacy would be to admit the truth of its establishment by Jesus Christ and its corollary, the truth of the Catholic Church. We have already shown here that Jesus did select Peter as head of the Apostles and gave him the keys to bind on both earth and in heaven (Mt 16:13-19). It has also been shown that since Christ intended His Church to be for all time, Peter had to have successors. That successor today, who goes back in an unbroken line to Peter, is the pope; this is an historical fact that anyone can determine and demonstrate.

Just as Jesus formed an apostolic college and appointed Peter as its head, who was to be the visible source of the unity that was to exist in His Church, so Peter's and the Apostles' successors are the perpetual and visible source of the unity Christ wills in His Church today. As Vatican Council II teaches (Constitution on the Church, 22): "The Roman Pontiff, by reason of his office as Vicar of Christ, namely, and as pastor of the entire Church, has full, supreme and universal power over the whole Church, a power which he can always exercise unhindered." This means that the pope is not like the chairman of a meeting or the presiding officer of a corporation; he has final and total power.

This power of the pope extends to two areas:

1. *Teaching Authority.* The pope is the supreme teacher in the Catholic Church in matters of faith and morals. When he teaches on faith and morals, his words and writings require filial respect and obedience by all members of the Church.

2. *Jurisdictional Authority.* This authority pertains to government and discipline within the Church. An example of this is the Apostolic Letter of Pope John Paul II in which he declares that it is by Christ's will that priestly ordination is reserved to men alone. The pope concluded this declaration by stating: "Wherefore, in order that all doubt may be removed regarding a matter of great importance, a matter which pertains to the Church's divine constitution itself, in virtue of my ministry of confirming the brethren (cf. Lk 22:32) I declare that the Church has no authority whatsoever to confer priestly ordination on women and this judgment is to be definitively held by all the Church's faithful." The matter of women's ordination which had been debated up to that point was from then on definitively closed.

When the pope speaks authoritatively, he does so from objective truth, which rejects subjectivism and relativism and which many use in being critical of the pope. Objective truth means that certain things are right or wrong in themselves, and no amount of reasoning or the best intention for doing them can make them right in themselves. An example of this is an abortion. God's command is "You shall not kill." The deliberate ending of human life, even though it is in the womb, even though it is in an early stage of growth, is a violation of God's commandment. All the specious slogans ("a woman's right to her body" or "a right to privacy"), all the specious emotional arguments ("back-alley abortions" or "a child destined for poverty"), all these are subjective and false arguments when judged against the eternal truth: "You shall not kill." When the Church, therefore, speaks on abortion, it does not do so from subjective sentimentality but from objective truth.

Infallibility

This brings us to the question of infallibility (incapability of error in matters of faith and morals) of pope and bishops in union with the pope. This is emphatically denied by those outside the Catholic Church and often misunderstood because it is believed it pertains to anything the pope says.

Again *Lumen Gentium*, 25 states: "The Roman Pontiff, head of the college of bishops, enjoys this infallibility in virtue of his office, when, as supreme pastor and teacher of all the faithful — who confirms his brethren in the faith (cf. Lk 22:32) — he proclaims in an absolute decision a doctrine pertaining to faith and morals. For that reason his definitions are rightly said to be irreformable by their very nature and not by reason of the assent of the Church, in as much as they were made with the assistance of the Holy Spirit promised to him in the person of blessed Peter himself. . . . For in such a case the Roman Pontiff does not utter a pronouncement as a private person, but rather does he expound and defend the teaching of the Catholic faith as the supreme teacher of the universal Church, in whom the Church's charism of infallibility is present in a singular way. The infallibility promised to the Church is also present in the body of bishops when, together with Peter's successor, they exercise the supreme teaching office."

The proof for infallibility in the matters of faith and morals is a Scriptural one and its reasoning goes like this:

1. Jesus intended to found a Church and make Peter its head (Mt 16:17-19). As head of the Church Peter was to confirm the Christians and to see that they received the doctrine Jesus taught and were properly guided (Jn 21:15-17).

2. Jesus promised that He would be with the Apostles and their successors for all time (Mt 28:18), so that they would be consecrated to truth (Jn 17:19). Jesus also promised that the Father would send the Holy Spirit to the Apostles so that the

Holy Spirit would guide them and make clear all that Jesus had revealed to them (Jn 14:26). That Holy Spirit was made visibly present on Pentecost Sunday (Acts 2:1-4).

3. Since Jesus promised to be with His Church for all times (Mt 28:20), the promises made to Peter and the Apostles had of necessity to be passed to their successors, pope and bishops.

4. Therefore, the presence of Jesus and the Holy Spirit in the Church is what keeps it from error. Infallibility is not merely a gift but a necessity since Jesus and the Holy Spirit always witness to the truth.

Roman Curia

The pope conducts the business of the Church through the Roman Curia which acts in the pope's name and by his authority for the good and services of the churches (canon 360). The Curia consists of congregations, tribunals, and offices. The congregations are headed by a cardinal prefect who has a committee of other cardinals and bishops to advise him. Congregations can have various offices responsible to the congregation. The congregations are: 1. for Bishops, 2. for Catholic Education, 3. for the Clergy, 4. for the Doctrine of the Faith, 5. for Oriental Churches, 6. for the Evangelization of Peoples. There are three tribunals in the Curia: 1. Apostolic Penitentiary for handling matters in the internal (conscience) forum and which grants dispensations, commutations, sanctions, and condonations; 2. Supreme Tribunal of the Apostolic Signatura. This is the supreme court in the external forum. It hears appeals from other court decisions, primarily those of the Roman Rota; 3. The Roman Rota is the court of First Instance in cases reserved to the pope or Holy See and it is also the tribunal of first appeal. It takes its name from the circular hall in which its judges first met.

Patriarchs

Patriarch (Greek *pater*, father; *archos*, chief) is a title given to a bishop who heads a see of apostolic origin and which has an ancient Liturgy. Patriarchs rank second to the pope in the hierarchy of jurisdiction. A patriarch is subject only to the pope and his authority goes beyond his immediate see and embraces all those who belong to his particular rite no matter where in the world they live. One of the pope's titles is Patriarch of the West. Eastern patriarchs exist for the Copts, Greek Melkites, Syrians, Maronites, Chaldeans, and Armenians. There is also a patriarch in Jerusalem for the Latin Rite. There are titular patriarchs (in name only) for Lisbon, Venice, the East Indies, and West Indies (now vacant).

Cardinals

A cardinal is a bishop chosen by the pope as an assistant and adviser in Church affairs. When a pope dies the college of cardinals meets and elects a successor. Some cardinals are engaged in full-time service in the Roman Curia, the administrative offices of the Church; others are bishops of dioceses around the world. They are called together from time to time to advise the pope on matters of Church doctrine and administration. Cardinals are appointed for life but only those under eighty years of age are allowed to be papal electors.

Archbishops

An archbishop (Greek *arch,* chief; *episkopus,* bishop) is one of a higher rank than a bishop. He is known as a *metropolitan archbishop* when he is placed over a number of suffragan sees. His see city is usually the most important city in an area. The Metropolitan Archbishop of New York, for example, has suffragan dioceses of Buffalo, Rochester, Syracuse, Ogdensburg, Albany, Brooklyn, and Rockville Centre. Usually the metropolitan's area is confined to a state but not always. For example, the Archdiocese of Hartford (Connecticut) also includes Providence (Rhode Island) as a suffragan see. The metropolitan archbishop has full authority in his own diocese but only influential authority in the suffragan dioceses, although he does take precedence over his suffragan bishops. He may call a provincial council and appeals from suffragan courts are referred to his courts.

There are other types of archbishops. *Coadjutor Archbishop* is an assistant bishop in an archdiocese who is appointed with the right of succession upon the resignation or death of the archbishop. A *Titular Archbishop* has the title of an archdiocese that no longer exists and has no archdiocesan jurisdiction. It is a title given to authorities in the Roman Curia, papal nuncios, and apostolic delegates. *Archbishop ad personam* is a title of honor given to some bishops for outstanding service to the Church. The late Archbishop Noll, Bishop of Fort Wayne, was given such a title in recognition for his service to the Church in founding Our Sunday Visitor. Finally, the title *Primate* is sometimes used for the archbishop of the original see in a country; for example, the Archbishop of Lima, Peru, is known as the Primate of Peru.

Bishops

A bishop is one who has received the fullness of the sacrament of holy orders and is held to be a successor of the Apostles. Only a bishop has the power to confer holy orders (episcopate, priesthood, diaconate). A bishop is a teacher, a shepherd, and an administrator. Collectively with the pope, bishops compose the Magisterium of the Catholic Church and when acting in unison with the pope can partake in infallibility. Bishops are subject to the pope, not in origin which is divine, but in the exercise of their power by virtue of their office. A bishop in charge of a diocese is the supreme authority in that diocese to whom clergy and laity give allegiance. The right to appoint bishops is reserved to the pope as head of the Church.

There are various types of bishops within the Church:

Ordinary or *Diocesan Bishop*. He is in charge of the diocese to which he is appointed and can be promoted or reassigned. *Eparch* is the title of a bishop in the Eastern Church. *Vicar General* is a title given to a deputy for the administration of a diocese; he may or may not be a bishop. *Coadjutor Bishop* is an assistant (auxiliary) bishop to an ordinary with right of succession. *Auxiliary Bishop* is a bishop who assists an ordinary; he may be a vicar for a particular area in the diocese. He is a titular bishop, that is one holding title to a diocese that no longer exists. Other titular bishops are appointed for various administrative roles within the Church. *Vicar Apostolic* is the ordinary for a region (vicariate) that has not yet been established as a diocese. His title is titular. *Prefect Apostolic* is the ordinary of a new area (prefecture) set up in the Church below that of a vicariate. He is usually not a bishop but one with the rank of Monsignor. There are other prelates, not bishops, who are actual or honorary members of the papal household and are given the title of Monsignor.

Priests

A priest is an ordained minister with power to celebrate the Eucharist (Mass), administer the sacraments of the Church (except holy orders), preach and teach the Gospel, impart blessings, and perform other functions assigned to him by his bishop or ecclesiastical superior. The term priest derives from the Greek *presbyteros*, elder. It is Catholic teaching that the priesthood is a sacrament instituted by Christ, that imparts an unending and sacred character on the soul. This character remains even if later the priest may be given permission to resign from the active priesthood. The priesthood of the New Testament traces itself back to the Levitical priesthood of the Old law. Priests are carefully trained in a Church-operated seminary (Latin *seminarium*, a seed plot) where the seminarian undergoes the equivalent of four years of college (philosophy major) and four years of university study (theology major). Often after ordination the priest can go on to higher or specialized studies before entering priestly duties.

Deacons

There are two types of deacons in the Catholic Church:

1. *Transitional Deacons.* Seminarians in their last year before priestly ordination are ordained to the transitional diaconate that is a path to the priesthood. As a deacon he is

The
Hierarchical Church

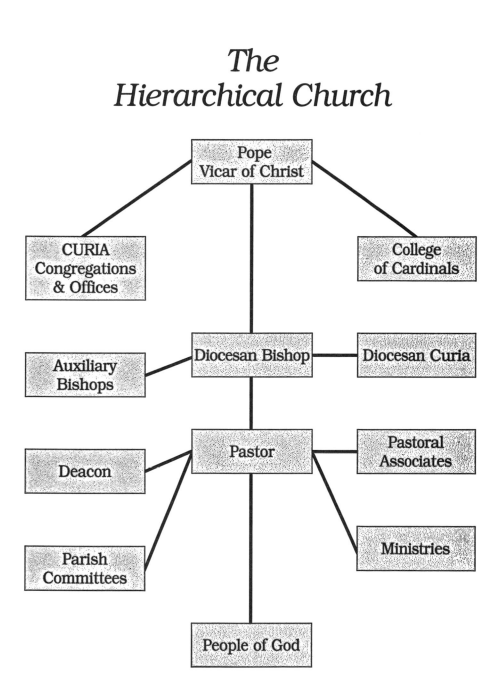

bound to the Liturgy of the Hours, the daily prayer of the Church, and according to Canon 1037 must publicly accept the obligation of celibacy. Ordination to the diaconate imprints a permanent mark on the soul.

2. *Permanent Deacons.* For many centuries the permanent diaconate fell into disuse within the Western Church until its restoration by Vatican Council II as a ministry of service. This order was established by the Apostles (Acts 6:1-6) who ordained the first seven deacons. A permanent deacon cannot marry after ordination; if married before, he cannot remarry if his wife dies.

In describing the hierarchical nature of the Church, the council in its Dogmatic Constitution on the Church (no. 29) described the restored ministry in this manner: "At the lower level of the hierarchy are to be found deacons, who receive the imposition of hands 'not unto the priesthood, but unto the ministry.' For strengthened by sacramental grace, they are dedicated to the People of God, in conjunction with the bishop and his body of priests, in the service of the liturgy, of the Gospel, and of works of charity. It pertains to the office of the deacon, in so far as it may be assigned to him by the competent authority, to administer Baptism solemnly, to be custodian and distributor of the Eucharist, in the name of the Church, to assist at and to bless marriages, to bring Viaticum to the dying, to read the sacred scripture to the faithful, to instruct and exhort the people, to preside over the worship and the prayer of the faithful, to administer sacramentals, and to officiate at funeral and burial services."

This then is the ministerial hierarchy in ranks and orders for the purpose of accomplishing Christ's mission to the world. It has been proven in almost 2,000 years of service to the people of God.

Review Questions

Explain the source of ministry in the Catholic Church.
What two kinds of authority does the pope have?
Prove that infallibility is scripturally based.
How is the Roman Curia organized?
Explain the difference between Cardinal, Patriarch, Archbishop, and Bishop.
What two kinds of deacons are there?

9. The Sacraments

Sacraments in General

The liturgical life of the Catholic Church is centered about its *seven sacraments.* A sacrament is an exterior sign instituted by Christ to give grace, and which requires the proper disposition of the one receiving it. Grace in turn is a supernatural gift bestowed by the Holy Spirit in order to aid the recipient's eternal salvation. It is the source of our justification and our participation in the life of God (C 1997). Grace is a gratuitous gift of God that makes of us a new creation (2 Cor 5:17). *Sanctifying grace* is received in baptism and is "an habitual gift" (C 2000) that "perfects the soul." It is distinguished from *actual grace* which refers to a particular intervention by God, whether at the beginning of conversion or in the course of the work of sanctification.

It is the teaching of the Catholic Church that its seven sacraments were instituted by Christ. This teaching is rooted in Sacred Scripture, Apostolic Tradition, and the teaching of the Church Fathers (C 1114). Three of the sacraments in addition to conferring grace also confer a character or seal on the soul and can be received only once. These three are baptism, confirmation, and holy orders. The purpose of the sacraments is to sanctify the recipient, to build up the Body of Christ, and to give worship to God.

Each sacrament is said to be *efficacious* because it is Christ Himself at work in the sacrament through the power of the Spirit. As the Catechism tells us (C 1127): "As fire transforms into itself everything it touches, so the Holy Spirit transforms into the divine life whatever is subjected to his power." Because of this action of the Holy Spirit, a sacrament is said to be effective by the very fact that the action is performed (*ex opere operato*).

Later we shall discuss the Liturgy, the action by which the life of worship is celebrated, particularly in the sacraments, but first let us consider each of the seven sacraments: baptism, confirmation, Eucharist, penance, anointing of the sick, holy orders, and matrimony. The first three mentioned are called the sacraments of Christian initiation (C 1212) because they are the foundation of Christian life. The next two are called sacraments of healing and the final two meant for a particular vocation in life.

I. Baptism

Baptism is the foundation on which Christian life is built, the door to life in the Spirit, and the path to the other sacraments. Through baptism we are freed of all sin and reborn as a son or daughter of God; also through baptism we are incorporated into the Church of Christ and made sharers in its mission. Baptism places an indelible mark on the soul and can only be received once. Every sacrament has matter and form and the matter of baptism is water applied in one of three ways: immersion, infusion (pouring), or aspersion (sprinkling). The form is:

> "I baptize you in the name of the Father and of the Son and of the Holy Spirit."

As long as the proper matter and form are used, baptism is valid in any Church or when performed by any person, including a lay person. Baptism takes its name from the Greek *baptizein*, meaning "to wash, dip, or immerse." The word explains the symbolism of the sacrament in which one dies with Christ (Rom 6:3) and rises with Him in resurrection as "a new creation" (2 Cor 5:17).

Baptism is necessary for salvation (Jn 3:5), but if baptism of water cannot be received, under particular circumstances, the Church recognizes baptism of blood (martyrdom for the Christian faith or a Christian virtue) or baptism of desire (perfect contrition plus a desire to do whatever God requires for salvation); however, these two types of baptism are not considered a sacrament. Because of the necessity of baptism, Jesus commanded His Church to take this sacrament to all the people of the world (Mt 28:19-20).

Infant baptism. Some Protestant groups deny baptism to

infants, limiting it only to those who can make a personal commitment "to be born again." Yet not a single such group can come up with any scriptural text for justification of its position. The Catholic Church has never denied infant baptism because it looks upon children as also being born of fallen human nature, tainted by original sin, and of need of new birth that will free them from the darkness of sin and give new life of grace as children of God. Spiritual growth begins at birth (1 Pt 2:1-5) and the Church holds as its mandate the wish of Jesus (Mk 10:14). "Let the children come to me; do not stop them; for it is to such as these that the kingdom of God belongs." There are historical records of the second century that show infant baptism was practiced and Scripture tells of Paul baptizing entire households (Acts 16:15, 18:8). Infant baptism does place an obligation for post-baptismal catechizing on parents, god-parents, and the Church itself for faith initiation and growth.

The effects of baptism (C 1262-1274). The sacrament of baptism signifies its effects, death, purification, regeneration, and renewal. These can be summarized under five headings:

1. Forgiveness of Sin. It has been defined by the Church that in baptism all sins are forgiven, original sin and personal sin, as well as any punishment due as reparation. In baptismal rebirth nothing remains that would impede entrance into the kingdom of God. While salvation has yet to be worked out and the consequences of sin remain (illness, suffering, death, and human concupiscence), baptism opens the channels of God's grace by which these human frailties can be met.

2. A New Creature. Baptism also makes the neophyte a new creation (2 Cor 5:17), an adopted child of God (Gal 4:5-7), member of Christ and co-heir with Him (Rom 8:17), and a temple of the Holy Spirit, justifying the person baptized and enabling that person to live a life of faith.

3. Entrance Into the Church. Baptism makes us members of the Church, incorporating us into the Mystical Body of Christ, wherein all accidental differences disappear and we all become brothers and sisters of one another and of the Lord. For as St. Paul tells us (1 Cor 12:13): "For in the one

Spirit we were all baptized into one body — Jews or Greeks, slaves or free — and we were all made to drink of one Spirit." Baptism enables us to share in the priesthood of Jesus Christ as St. Peter says (1 Pt 2:9): "You are a chosen race, a royal priesthood, a holy nation, God's own people, in order that you may proclaim the mighty acts of him who called you out of darkness into his marvelous light."

Baptism bestows upon the one baptized both rights and obligations. As the Catechism (1269) summarizes, "the baptized person also enjoys rights within the Church: to receive the sacraments, to be nourished with the Word of God and to be sustained by the other spiritual helps of the Church." Baptism also imposes obligations and duties upon the one baptized, among these are to live the teachings of Christ; to serve our brothers and sisters in faith; to "obey your [church] leaders and submit to them" (Heb 13:17), holding them in respect and affection (1 Thes 5:12); to observe the commandments and laws of the Church; to profess one's faith before others; and to participate in the missionary vocation of the Church.

4. Sacramental Bond of Unity. Vatican Council II in its Decree on Ecumenism states that "the restoration of unity among all Christians is one of the principal concerns" of the council. The decree goes on to note that the foundation for this total unity already exists, stating (no. 3), those who "believe in Christ and have been properly baptized are put in some, though imperfect, communion with the Catholic Church." Recognizing that obstacles exist, the decree nevertheless concludes, "But even in spite of them it remains true that all who have been justified by faith in baptism are incorporated into Christ; they therefore have a right to be called Christians, and with good reason are accepted as brothers [and sisters] by the children of the Catholic Church. . . . Baptism, therefore, constitutes the sacramental bond of unity existing among all who through it are reborn" (no. 22).

5. An Indelible Spiritual Mark. Baptism imprints on the soul a spiritual mark (character) that cannot be removed (2 Cor 1:22) and no action or person can erase that mark. Even though the baptized may drift away from Christ, that person will always be marked as belonging to Christ. It is for this reason that baptism cannot be repeated.

II. Confirmation

If baptism starts new life in the Church, confirmation is its strengthening. Confirmation is a sacrament of the New Law wherein the recipient receives the Holy Spirit through the anointing with the oil of chrism by the bishop (or his delegate) in the form of a cross on the forehead, the imposition of hands (matter) while saying the words (form), "Be sealed with the gift of the Holy Spirit."

Confirmation is the second of the sacraments of initiation, completing baptismal grace, and can only be given to one who has been baptized. Like baptism, confirmation prints an indelible character or seal on the soul. This character perfects the common priesthood of the faithful. Preparation should be made for the reception and one should be in the state of grace, with penance beforehand if necessary. The bishop is the ordinary minister of the sacrament and the priest an extraordinary minister when delegated by the bishop. It is a sacrament instituted by Christ (Acts 1:5) and was conferred by the Apostles (Acts 8:14-17). In the early Church the sacrament was called "laying on of hands" (Heb 6:2) and its present name given because it strengthens or confirms the soul by the infusion of divine grace.

In the Eastern Church confirmation is celebrated together with baptism. This was the early practice in the entire Church, conferring what St. Cyprian called a "double sacrament." In the Western Church it became the practice to defer the sacrament in order to obtain a personal commitment and to express the communion of the recipient with the bishop as guarantor of the unity, catholicity, and apostolicity of his Church and as a sign of descent from the apostolic Church. However, even in the Western Church the sacrament is conferred on an adult immediately following baptism, and then to be followed by the first reception of the Eucharist.

The *effect* of confirmation is the outpouring of the Holy Spirit, as took place for the Apostles on the first Pentecost day. According to the *Catechism of the Catholic Church* (1303), confirmation brings an increase and deepening of baptismal grace and:

— it roots us more deeply in the divine filiation which makes us cry, "Abba! Father!",
— it unites us more firmly to Christ,
— it increases the gifts of the Holy Spirit in us,
— it renders our bond with the Church more perfect,
— it gives us a special strength of the Holy Spirit to spread and defend the faith by word and action as true witnesses of Christ, to confess the name of Christ boldly, and never to be ashamed of the Cross.

III. The Eucharist

The Eucharist (Greek *eucharistia*, thanksgiving) is the highest of all the Christian sacraments and the apex of Catholic Liturgy, for it is Christ Himself who is contained in it. It takes its name from the prayer of thanksgiving offered by Christ at the Last Supper when He established this sacrament and ordered it continued in memory of Him (Lk 22:17-19). It is the last sacrament of Christian initiation. Like the Trinity or the Incarnation, it is a mystery which the mind cannot comprehend but one to which assent is given because of trust and faith in Christ's own word. It is the eternal sacrifice of the New Law in which the sacrifice of the Cross is perpetually offered to the Father. In the Mass Jesus does not die again but the Eucharist is "a memorial of his death and resurrection: a sacrament of love, a sign of unity, a bond of charity . . . 'in which Christ is consumed, the mind is filled with grace, and a pledge of future glory is given to us' " (C 1323).

To understand properly the scriptural background of this sacrament one should read chapter six of John's Gospel and the institution accounts at the Last Supper in each of the Synoptic (Matthew, Mark, and Luke) Gospels. This scriptural background will be explained in more detail as this treatment proceeds.

The sacrament of the Eucharist is referred to by a number

of other names, each of which gives an insight into this Sacrament:

The Lord's Supper because it originated in the Last Supper in which Jesus celebrated the pasch with His Apostles on the night of His arrest. It is a term St. Paul used (1 Cor 11:20).

Breaking of the Bread, a term used in the apostolic Church which derived from the account of Jesus (Mk 14:22) breaking bread at the Last Supper and the source of His recognition by the disciples of Emmaus (Lk 24:30-31). The early Christians understood that by sharing in the Bread, they entered into communion with Jesus and became one body with Him (1 Cor 10:17).

Memorial of Christ's passion and resurrection in response to the command of Jesus (Lk 22:19).

Eucharistic Assembly because Catholics assemble each Sunday for the eucharistic rite. This is also known as the *Divine Liturgy*, the *Sacrifice of the Mass*, or simply the *Mass*, a common name for the sacrifice which derived from the Latin dismissal, "Ite, missa est" (Go, the Mass is ended), which in turn was a reminder that Christians were sent on a mission to show the love and life of Christ.

Holy Communion, the Sacred Species themselves, or the sharing through Holy Communion one's life with that of Christ and all other communicants to form a single body (1 Cor 10:16-17).

The *Blessed Sacrament,* extolling both the sacredness of the sacrament itself and the name for the Eucharist that is reserved in the tabernacle.

Bread of Life in which we partake in the divine life of Jesus and find sustenance for our own spiritual life.

Mystery of the Altar by which we recognize an unexplainable truth revealed to us by Jesus in whom there is no deceit.

Eucharist Prefigured. There is an old adage that "coming events cast their shadow before." This is certainly true in Scripture. The bread and wine of the Eucharist were prefigured in the Old Testament. In Genesis 14:18 we read of the bread and wine offered to Abraham by the priest Melchizedek. The Jewish Passover meal has unleavened bread to remind its celebrants of the haste in which their ancestors left Egypt and the wine's "cup of blessing" at the end has a messianic aspect. The manna in the desert was a bread of life for the fleeing Jews. At the start of His public life, Jesus turned water into wine foreshadowing the wine that would become His Blood. In the two miracles of the feeding of the thousands, Jesus blessed a few loaves, broke them and then fed the multitudes, as would His own Body and Blood.

Jesus Reveals the Eucharist. In the New Testament Jesus reveals Himself as a masterful teacher who well understood the working of the human mind. He caught the attention of people through His miracles and revelations. He taught them through stories (parables) with which they were familiar. To reveal His teaching on the Eucharist, He prepared by two dramatic miracles — the feeding of the four thousand (Mk 8:1-10) and of the five thousand (Jn 6:1-14). After this second miracle, the people realizing the sign He had wrought began to say, "This is indeed the prophet who is to come into the world."

The sixth chapter of John goes on to recount that the crowd came out again to Him the next day, expecting to be fed again and looking for another sign. Jesus tells them that they must believe in Him.

"What sign are you going to give us then, so that we may see it and believe in you?" people ask. They remind Him of the manna Moses gave the people in the desert.

Jesus corrects them, telling them it was not Moses who gave manna but His Father in heaven, adding, "For the bread of God is that which comes down from heaven and gives life to the world."

"Sir," they respond, "give us this bread always."

"I am the bread of life," Jesus replies. "Whoever comes to me will never be hungry, and whoever believes in me will never be thirsty."

The people began to murmur among themselves about Jesus' implication that He came down from heaven. Up to this point one could say that Jesus was only speaking symbolically, likening Himself to a gift from God. But he corrects this impression, stating, "I am the living bread that came down from heaven. Whoever eats of this bread will live forever; and the bread that I will give for the life of the world is my flesh."

Even to this point one could argue that Jesus was speaking in symbols, using bread from heaven to mean the word of God and the giving of His flesh to the crucifixion death that awaited him. The Jewish crowd, however, began to think He was serious and the question was raised, "How can this man give us his flesh to eat?"

Jesus at this point, seeing that He was losing some of the people, could have said that He was not speaking literally. Instead He spoke even more directly and emphatically:

"Very truly, I tell you, unless you eat the flesh of the Son of Man and drink His blood, you have no life in you. Those who eat my flesh and drink my blood have eternal life, and I will raise them up on the last day; for my flesh is true food and my blood is true drink. Those who eat my flesh and drink my blood abide in me, and I in them."

This teaching scandalized His hearers and even some of His own followers turned away and left Him because they could not accept it. Jesus' intention of literalness is revealed when He turns to His Apostles and asks, "Do you also wish to go away?"

Simon Peter answered for the Apostles: "Lord, to whom can we go? You have the words of eternal life. We have come to believe and know that you are the Holy One of God."

In His revelation of the Eucharist, Jesus spoke of "the bread that I *will* give," indicating that the establishment of the Eucharist was to be at a future date. That future came at the Last Supper on the night before Jesus was put to death. Mark (14:22-24) describes it in this way:

> While they were eating, he took a loaf of bread, and after blessing it he broke it, gave it to them, and said, "Take, this is my body." Then he took a cup, and after giving thanks he gave it to them, and all of them drank from it. He said to them, "This is my blood of the covenant, which is poured out for many."

Luke (22:19-20) gives this account:

> Then he took a loaf of bread, and when he had given thanks, he broke it and gave it to them, saying, "This is my body, which is given for you. Do this in remembrance of me." And he did the same with the cup after supper, saying, "This cup that is poured out for you is the new covenant in my blood."

Christ's command "Do this" clearly shows that He was instituting a rite that He wanted carried on. The apostolic Church accepted this command as St. Paul tells us (1 Cor 11:23-27):

> For I received from the Lord what I also handed on to you, that the Lord Jesus on the night when he was betrayed took a loaf of bread, and when he had given thanks, he broke it and said, "This is my body which is for you. Do this in remembrance of me." In the same way also the cup, after supper, saying, "This cup is the new covenant in my blood. Do this, as often as you drink it, in remembrance of me."

Then Paul adds a warning that many seem to ignore (vv. 27-29):

> Whoever, therefore, eats the bread or drinks the cup of the Lord in an unworthy manner will be answerable for the body and blood of the Lord. Examine yourselves, and only then eat of the bread and drink of the cup. For all who eat and drink without discerning the body, eat and drink judgment against themselves.

From the Gospel texts come the words of consecration used at Mass. The bread and wine are the matter of the sacrament and the consecration words are the form. For almost two thousand years Catholics have been celebrating the eucharistic sacrifice, passed on from Jesus through the Apostles. When the Protestant revolt came, the Mass was rejected by most. High Anglicans (Episcopalians) have preserved the rite. Lutherans believe in the words of Christ and interpret them closely to the Catholic Church, their interpretation for what happens being called *transignification.*

Catholics use the term *transubstantiation* and there is a difference in meaning.

On the other hand most Protestants, who call themselves people of the Book and boast "Scripture alone!" ignore the literalness of Scripture and at best, often only occasionally, commemorate a symbolic Last Supper, never a reality, and in effect deny the words of Jesus.

But for Catholics, their doctrine is expressed: "The celebration of the Eucharist is the center of the entire Christian life, both for the Church universal and for the local congregations of the Church. The other sacraments, all the ministries of the Church, and the works of the apostolate are united with the Eucharist and directed toward it. For the Holy Eucharist contains the entire spiritual treasure of the Church, that is, Christ himself, our passover and living bread' " (*Eucharisticum Mysterium*, 6).

Holy Communion. The obligatory celebration of the Eucharist, which binds all Catholics under pain of serious sin, takes place on each Sunday and holy day of the year. Daily Mass (except for Good Friday) is celebrated in all the parishes of the world at which many of the faithful attend. A part of the Mass is the sacred banquet (C 1382) of communion in which the faithful take part in response to the Lord's admonition (Jn 6:53): "Very truly, I tell you, unless you eat the flesh of the Son of Man and drink his blood, you have no life in you." The people reply to the Lord's invitation, "Take and eat" by responding together in words based upon Scripture (Mt 8:8): "Lord, I am not worthy to receive you, but only say the word, and I shall be healed." When the communicant comes forward, the minister holds up the Sacred Bread and says, "Body of Christ." The communicant's "Amen" is a statement of belief in the reality of the Eucharist. The action is repeated with the Sacred Blood. The Church teaches that Jesus is wholly sacramentally present under each species and the reception under one alone makes it possible to receive total eucharistic grace. The Church also teaches, the sign of communion "has a fuller form when it is received under both kinds" (*Eucharisticum Mysterium*, 32).

Eucharistic Devotions

Perpetual adoration. This devotion is observed by some religious communities, such as the Sacramentine Nuns, where the Blessed Sacrament is exposed in a monstrance on the altar and adored day and night.

Eucharistic devotion. Weekday parish exposition of the Blessed Sacrament, usually after the morning Mass and reposition taking place in the evening. During the day people of the parish take turns in adoration.

Holy hour. Often monthly on the First Friday but also on other occasions, an hour is given to adoration of the exposed Sacrament, with hymns, Scripture readings, homily, meditation, prayers, and concluding with Benediction.

Benediction. A paraliturgical service in which the Blessed Sacrament is exposed for reverence, and consisting of hymns and prayers, with a blessing being given with the Sacrament before it is reposed in the tabernacle.

Processions. A procession formed by the people in which the minister carries the Sacrament in a monstrance. These are frequently held on the feast of the Body and Blood of Christ but also at other times.

Eucharistic congress. An international gathering of Catholics from all parts of the world to honor the Blessed Sacrament and presided over by a papal legate. It consists of Masses, processions, Benedictions, sermons, and seminars all centered on the Blessed Sacrament with the aim of increasing devotion. Similar meetings can be held on national and regional levels.

The Fruits of Holy Communion

Holy Communion augments our union with Jesus. The Lord has told us (Jn 6:56), "He who eats my flesh and drinks my blood abides in me, and I in him." Union with Jesus should be the goal of every Christian and the substantial union brought about through the reception of the Eucharist is the most intimate and grace-giving. We recall Christ's words (Jn 15:5): "Apart from me you can do nothing."

Holy Communion unites Christians. Through Holy

Communion we are united substantially to Jesus and to all others who partake of the Eucharist. This includes the members of Eastern Churches not in union with Rome but which do have valid sacraments. Nevertheless the Decree on Ecumenism reminds us that "of its very nature, celebration of the Eucharist signifies the fullness of profession of faith and the fullness of ecclesial communion." Hence by Church regulation, the Eucharist cannot be given to non-Catholics except in very restricted and particular cases.

Holy Communion is the food of spiritual growth. Just as the body needs physical food to grow and remain well, so too must the soul be spiritually nourished. Holy Communion "preserves, increases, and renews the life of grace received at Baptism" (C 1392).

Holy Communion strengthens us against sin. The Blood of Jesus was poured out for the forgiveness of sin (Mt 26:28) and by uniting ourselves with it, we receive strength against sin. As we grow closer to Jesus, the more difficult it is to break away from Him by serious sin.

Requisites for the Mass

Following the example of Jesus at the Last Supper, the bread used for the Eucharist must be made from wheat in accordance with the tradition of the entire Church; it must be unleavened in accord with the tradition of the Latin Church.

The wine used for the Eucharist must be made from the fruit of the grape vine, natural and pure, unmixed with anything else.

The sacred vessels used at Mass should be made of materials that are solid, not easily breakable, and esteemed as valuable in the region where they are to be used.

In summary, as St. Thomas Aquinas says, "The Eucharist is the Sacrament of sacraments and all other sacraments are ordered to it as to their end." We have shown that the Eucharist is Christ's great gift to His Church. We end this section with a prayer that we may one day be joined to our now separated brethren in the eucharistic Body of Christ.

Review Questions

What is a sacrament?

Name the sacraments of initiation, of healing, of the states of life.

Justify infant baptism.

What are the effects of baptism?

What are the effects of confirmation?

How does confirmation differ in East and West?

By what other names is the Eucharist called?

Why do Catholics believe in the reality of the Eucharist as the true Body and Blood of Jesus? Give scriptural proofs.

What are the fruits of Holy Communion?

What does my "Amen" at receiving Communion mean?

IV. Penance

The three sacraments thus far discussed are called sacraments of initiation, because they are means through which we receive new life in Christ. The next two to be discussed are referred to as sacraments of healing. We are imperfect vessels, subject to both spiritual and physical ills. Jesus, who understood our human nature because He shared in it, left behind two sacraments — penance and anointing of the sick — to meet these ills.

The sacrament of penance is also known by a number of other titles which give an insight into the nature of this sacrament.

Sacrament of reconciliation. Sin, so common to the human condition, separates us from God. Serious (mortal) sin cuts us off from God's grace because it is a renunciation of God's domain over His human creation. For those who do fall into sin, St. Paul exhorts (2 Cor 5:20), "We entreat you on behalf of Christ, be reconciled to God." Through the sacrament of penance the sinner is reconciled once again to God.

Sacrament of conversion. When Jesus began His public life, His message was one of repentance for sin (Mk 1:15). It was a call for personal conversion. By sin we stray away from God and need to turn around our lives and be reconverted to

Him. We do so through this sacrament in which the past is forgiven and a new start made.

Sacrament of confession. An essential element of the sacrament is the disclosure of our sins to the priest, who receives our purpose of amendment and conversion, prescribes a penance to be done, and in the name of Christ (Jn 20:23) forgives the sins, granting to the penitent "pardon and peace."

Difficulties

Most Protestants have difficulty in accepting this sacrament. Its rejection was a key element for the Protestant Reformers. Their heirs today are the product of long conditioning. In justification of their belief, they quote St. Paul (1 Tm 2:5): "There is also one mediator between God and men, the man Christ Jesus." No Catholic would disagree with that quotation. It is the heart of Paul's theology that Jesus Christ is the Father's appointed mediator, the center of God's plan of salvation, the Redeemer who satisfied for our sins. But that does not prevent Jesus from choosing others to assist Him in the work of mediation. As has been shown He chose the Apostles who were to have successors who would continue assisting Jesus. The role of the Apostles and their successors is only a secondary role for they have no power of themselves but only when acting in the place of Jesus and in the name of Jesus. In the matter of forgiveness for sin, the Church extends this delegated power to its validly ordained priests, a right granted the Church by Jesus (Mt 16:19).

The Apostles recognized this right that had been given them and they passed it on to their successors and their delegates. In his homily on Leviticus, Origen wrote c. AD 240 in praise of the Catholic "who does not shrink to confess his sins to a priest of the Lord." About the same time, St. Cyprian, writing on faults, told Christians to "confess to the priests of God in an honest way and in sorrow, making an open disclosure of conscience."

Often when discussing confession with a Protestant the objection is made, "But I can confess my sins directly to God."

Of course one can. And the person's sins will be forgiven, provided there is true repentance for alienation from God and a firm purpose of amendment to avoid these sins in the future. But can the person be certain that the proper disposition for the forgiveness of sins is present? Is there absolute certainty that the sins are forgiven? Jesus gave a method by which we might know for sure — the sacrament of penance, which He ordained as the ordinary way for the forgiveness of sin and a method that gives the certainty of forgiveness through the absolution of the priest (Jn 20:23). As the Catechism (1446) tells us, "Christ instituted the sacrament of Penance for all sinful members of his Church: above all for those who, since Baptism, have fallen into grave sin, and have thus lost their baptismal grace and wounded ecclesial communion. It is to them that the sacrament of Penance offers a new possibility to convert and to recover the grace of justification."

The certainty of Catholics concerning the power of the priest to absolve from sin is founded in the grant from Christ, given on the night of His resurrection, as related in the Gospel of John (20:19-23). The key words are:

"Receive the Holy Spirit. If you forgive the sins of any, they are forgiven them; if you retain the sins of any, they are retained."

One either accepts these words of Jesus or rejects them, and, if the latter, then the whole of Scripture must be discarded and the whole of Christianity is meaningless.

Jesus was given the power by the Father "to execute judgment" (Jn 5:27) in the matter of sin (Mt 9:6). It was this power He was passing on to the Apostles and through them to their successors. The Church has the right (Mt 16:19) to determine how this power will be used. There is a difference between these two powers. That given to Peter as head of the Church was a broad power that concerned faith and morals. Peter could in no way contradict the teachings of Jesus; he had to uphold them. But in those matters in which there was no teaching, in matters of moral discipline, Peter's decision was the same as if Christ decided. The power given to the

Apostles was a limited power, restricted solely to the forgiveness of sin. That it was to be a sacrament, a sign, is indicated by the conferring of the Spirit (*pneuma*, breath, spirit), John using the same Greek word as is used in the Greek version of the Genesis account (2:7) of the creation of man.

One should not be surprised at the concern of Jesus about sin. Freedom from sin was the basis of His mission. Mark gave us the rallying cry of Jesus at the beginning of his Gospel (1:15): "Repent, and believe in the good news." Repentance means to turn away from sin; it is the beginning of conversion, and conversion is an ongoing process. Conversion is more than being "born again," for belief is empty without deeds. We are all sinners, and we must not delude ourselves into thinking sin does not matter. As 1 John 1:8-10 tells us about confession, "If we say that we have no sin, we deceive ourselves, and the truth is not in us. If we confess our sins, he who is faithful and just will forgive us our sins and cleanse us from all unrighteousness. If we say we have not sinned, we make him a liar, and his word is not in us." Jesus gave us the sacrament of penance as a certain means to reconcile ourselves with His Father and with His Church.

In the early Church grave sins committed after baptism were considered not only an offense to God but to the unity of the Christian community. Public penance, often severe and lengthy, was required. Irish monks, following the Eastern monastic tradition, instituted a private form of penance in their communities and among the people they served. When as missioners they carried the faith to northern Europe, they introduced this private form of reconciliation, which rapidly became the norm and is used to this day. Although the priest is the minister, it is God the Father who forgives sins, as the absolution used in the Latin Church shows:

"God, the Father of mercies,
through the death and resurrection of His Son
has reconciled the world to Himself
and sent the Holy Spirit among us

> for the forgiveness of sins;
> through the ministry of the Church
> may God give you pardon and peace,
> and I absolve you from your sins
> in the name of the Father,
> and of the Son,
> and of the Holy Spirit."

The confession of sins is the matter of the sacrament of penance and the absolution by the priest is its form.

To prepare oneself for confession a careful examination of conscience should be made. The penitent is required to confess all serious (mortal) sins and it is recommended that what the Catechism (1458) calls "everyday faults" (venial sins) be confessed as these hinder one's progress in spiritual growth. Mortal sins should not be allowed to remain on the soul because they can have fatal and eternal consequences. To ensure this the law of the Church (canon law 989) requires that Catholics who have reached the age of reason confess serious sins at least once a year. The Church recommends that the sacrament be approached at least monthly, even if no serious sins exist.

The penitent is expected to bring certain dispositions to the sacrament (C 1450). There must be a *willingness* to confess all serious sins. There should be *sorrow* for sin; preferably perfect sorrow, which arises from having given offense to God; but imperfect sorrow (fear of damnation or of some punishment) is sufficient. This sorrow is known as contrition. *Conversion* of life is a requisite. Confession is not permission to go out and start sinning all over again. One has to resolve to amend one's life, to try to avoid the confessed sins in the future. Conversion of life requires that one make *satisfaction* for wrongs committed (e.g., restore stolen goods or their value, or undo slander). Satisfaction also requires the acceptance of the *penance assigned* by the priest; this can be prayer, a work of mercy, some sacrifice, or whatever the priest would deem worthy. Finally, all these dispositions are summed up in the *Act of Contrition* the penitent recites immediately before receiving *absolution.*

Celebration of the Sacrament. The *ordinary* way of receiving the sacrament of penance is in private confession. The penitent approaches the priest in the confessional or another suitable place, is greeted and blessed by the confessor, exhorted to repentance, makes the confession, receives advice and an assigned penance by the priest, makes an Act of Contrition, is given absolution, and dismissed by the confessor.

The sacrament can also be celebrated in a communal setting (C 1482). This is common in parishes in Lent and Advent in preparation for Easter and Christmas. A typical celebration would include an opening hymn, reading from Scripture followed by a homily, a general examination of conscience, instructions, and *individual* confessions. Usually a number of priests are brought in to hear confessions.

In case of *grave* necessity, a communal celebration of reconciliation may be held with general confession and absolution. Canon 961 gives two examples: 1. When danger of death is imminent (e.g., from war, plague, some natural disaster and there is not time for confessions to be heard); 2. When a serious necessity exists because of the number of penitents and a supply of confessors is not readily available and the people would be deprived of the sacrament for *a long time*. However, the canon specifies that the diocesan bishop must decide whether such conditions exist (canon 961:2) and it is not up to an individual confessor. Moreover, people who are absolved are held to make an individual confession when a priest is available. The canon also specifies that crowds for some feast or pilgrimage would not come under this exception to the ordinary means of confession.

The Catechism (1484) citing the Order of Penance states: "'Individual, integral confession and absolution remain the only ordinary way for the faithful to reconcile themselves with God and the Church, unless physical or moral impossibility excuses from this kind of confession.' There are profound reasons for this. Christ is at work in each of the sacraments. He personally addresses every sinner: 'My son, your sins are forgiven you' [Mk 2:5]. He is the physician tending each one of the sick who need him to cure them. He raises them up and reintegrates them into fraternal communion."

Seal of the Confessional. A confessor is obliged to maintain absolute secrecy concerning facts learned through sacramental confession. He can make no use of the knowledge given him or reveal anything concerning the confession by word, action, or behavior. A confessor who directly violates the seal of confession incurs automatic excommunication. This canon would also bind an interpreter or one who overheard the confession. This excommunication can only be removed by the Holy See.

Excommunication. The most severe penalty that the Church imposes for wrongdoing is excommunication (C 1463). This severs one from the life of the Church. It denies the reception of the sacraments and cuts one off from certain ecclesiastical acts. There are nine offenses that incur excommunication, seven of them are automatic (*Latae sententiae*, LS) which means they incur the penalty by the very commission of the act and require no judicial judgment. These are:

1. Apostasy, heresy, or schism (LS).
2. Violation of the Blessed Eucharist (LS).
3. Physical attack on the pope (LS).
4. Confessional absolution of an accomplice (LS).
5. Pretended celebration of Eucharist or conferral of sacramental absolution by one not a priest.
6. Unauthorized episcopal consecration (LS).
7. Direct violation of confessional seal by confessor (LS).
8. Violation of confessional seal by interpreter or others.
9. All involved in a deliberate abortion (LS).

Indulgences. Closely associated with the sacrament of penance are indulgences, a matter greatly misunderstood by many outside the Church, some even going so far as to think an indulgence is permission to commit sin. Pope Paul VI in his constitution The Doctrine of Indulgences defines an indulgence this way: "An indulgence is a remission before God of the temporal punishment due to sins whose guilt has already been forgiven, which the faithful Christian who is duly disposed gains under certain prescribed conditions through the actions of the Church which, as the minister of redemption, dispenses and applies with authority the treasury of the satisfactions of Christ and the saints."

An indulgence is called partial or plenary (full) according to whether it removes part or all temporal punishment due to sin. It is also Church teaching that an indulgence can be applied to the living (oneself) or the dead. An indulgence is only granted by the performance of some good and meritorious action in works of devotion, penance, and charity. To gain an indulgence one must be in the state of grace (i.e., free from mortal sin), and in the case of a plenary indulgence, confession, reception of Communion, and prayer for the pope are required.

A person outside the Catholic Church might properly ask, "Where does the Church get such power?" The answer is that the Church received this power from Jesus Christ when He bestowed on it the power of binding and loosening (Mt 16:19). To understand the Church's teaching on indulgences, one must understand other Church doctrines on the effects of sin, purgatory, the treasury of the Church, and the Communion of Saints.

The Effects of Sin. Every sin has a double effect. First, sin alienates us from God to a greater or lesser degree. Serious (mortal) sin makes a complete alienation in which communion with God is broken (C 1472). Mortal sin renders us incapable of life with God and if one dies in it, eternal separation from God is the result. Mortal sin destroys charity in the heart. Mortal sin involves grave matter, e.g., the Ten Commandments, and requires full knowledge of what one is doing, and deliberate and full consent to do it despite knowing it is wrong. Mortal sin breaks our covenant with God.

Venial sin does not involve complete alienation from God, although it affects and wounds charity in the heart (C 1855). Venial sin shows a disordered affection for created goods, impedes the soul's progress in acquiring virtue, and its frequent commission can dispose us to mortal sin. Venial sin shows an unhealthy attachment to things of this life, and if one dies in this state, it does require temporal punishment. One can be freed from this temporal punishment by conversion to God, atonement, and purification of attachment to things of this world. Many people do die in the state of sanctity and the Church recognizes this in the examination of the lives of some of its members whom it names as saints. But for most death comes before purification is complete and hence the soul goes to a place of final purification called purgatory.

Purgatory. Purgatory is a red flag for many people outside the Church. They assert that it is a man-made doctrine that is never mentioned in Scripture. It is true that one will not find the word "purgatory" in Scripture but then neither will one find the words "Trinity" or "Incarnation" which are basic doctrines of Christianity. The subject of purgatory is implied in Scripture and its necessity is shown there. In the discussion above on the effects of sin, it was shown that the mercy of God will grant forgiveness of sin but the effects of sin must still be atoned for before we can enter heaven. Either this must be done in this life or after death in a place of atonement which the Church calls purgatory because it is a place where one is purged or cleansed from the effects of sin.

Jesus tells us that it is the pure of heart who will see God (Mt 5:8). The Book of Revelation (21:27) tells us that nothing unclean can enter heaven. This means that when we die if we are to enter heaven immediately, we must be in a state of relative perfection. "Yet," as I wrote in *Answering a Fundamentalist,* "few of us die perfect, and perfection is necessary if we are to be in the presence of All-Perfection. Most of us die with some attachment to sin. We die with our pride, our failures in charity, our lack of prayerfulness, our human weaknesses. These are small defects, not willed as an alienation from God, or cause for us to be sent to an eternity in hell, but defects nevertheless that must be removed if we are to enter the abode of saints. The place where the removal of these defects takes place we call purgatory."

There are a number of allusions in Scripture that refer to purgatory as a purifying fire. The notion of purgatory antedated Jesus and existed long before the Catholic Church came into existence. In the Second Book of Maccabees (12:46) we read of a collection taken up by the Jewish leader, Judas Maccabeus, to be sent to Jerusalem to obtain prayers for those who had fallen in battle in order to make "atonement for the dead, so that they might be delivered from their sin." If these fallen soldiers were already condemned to hell, prayer would have been useless. If they were in heaven, prayer would be unnecessary. What Judas Maccabeus was implying is that they were in an intermediate place undergoing atonement. Whether you call this intermediate place *sheol* or *place of atonement* or *purgatory* does not matter.

The Church has never defined how long one remains in purgatory and this is open to theological speculation. The existence of purgatory is not. As Sirach advises us (7:33), "Do not withhold kindness even from the dead." So Catholics pray for their deceased, sacrifice for them, and gain indulgences in their behalf in order that the departed may more swiftly gain their goal of visible union with the Father and Son.

Communion of Saints (C 1474). The Church's teaching on indulgences is closely allied to its teaching on the Communion of Saints which Pope Leo XIII described as "the mutual sharing of help, expiation, prayers, and benefits among the faithful who, whether they are already in possession of their heavenly fatherland or are detained in purgatory or are still living as pilgrims on earth, are united and form one commonwealth, whose head is Christ, whose form is charity." This Communion of Saints is shared in by all Christians, not only Catholics. The Church is composed of three levels: the Church Militant, those of us who are still working out our salvation here on earth; the Church Suffering, those in purgatory who are still awaiting full salvation; and the Church Triumphant, those in heaven with the Lord. Each level can aid the other two. We can pray and sacrifice for the souls in purgatory; the saints in heaven can pray for us, and we can request their prayers.

Treasury of the Church (C 1476). This term does not refer to material wealth but to a spiritual treasury of "infinite value, which can never be exhausted" because it was brought about by the infinite merits gained by its founder, Jesus Christ, for the purpose that humanity could be set free from sin and have eternal communion with God. To this treasury is added the merits gained by all the saints, who have made their own lives holy and carried out the mission the Father entrusts to us. By their lives they not only won their own salvation but gained a surplus of merit that can be used by their brothers and sisters in Christ. In granting indulgences, the Church draws upon this infinite merit while encouraging the Church on earth to works of devotion, piety, and charity.

Review Questions

Prove that Jesus established the sacrament of penance.
Why is penance essential to the mission of Christ?
How should one prepare for confession?
What penalty applies to the Seal of Confession?
Name some automatic excommunications.
What is an indulgence?
What are the effects of sin?
Explain the logic of purgatory.
What is the Communion of Saints?
What composes the treasury of the Church?

V. Anointing of the Sick

Jesus established this sacrament when he sent His Apostles forth on a mission of repentance (Mk 6:7-13) and the Apostles "anointed with oil many who were sick and cured them." St. James described the power of this sacrament (Jas 5:14-15): "Are any among you sick? They should call for the elders of the church and have them pray over them, anointing them with oil in the name of the Lord. The prayer of faith will save the sick, and the Lord will raise them up; and anyone who has committed sins will be forgiven."

What James is referring to is the sacrament of the anointing of the sick as practiced by the Catholic Church in which sins are forgiven and bodily health prayed for. The recipients of this sacrament are Christians suffering serious illness, and persons with infirmities due to old age. The sacrament can be repeated for a new illness or if the person is in danger again from the same illness. The matter of the sacrament is the anointing with oil and the form is the prayer of anointing:

"Through this holy anointing may the Lord in His love and mercy help you with the grace of the Holy Spirit. May the Lord who frees you from sin save you and raise you up."

In carrying out this sacrament the Church is following the example and command of Jesus. The Gospels are full of Christ's concern for the sick and the many miracles He worked in their behalf. He passed this concern on to His Apostles, telling them, "Cure the sick." Jesus identified Himself with the sick and suffering for as Isaiah tells us (53:4) "he has borne our infirmities and carried our diseases."

There is a great misunderstanding of suffering and illness in the world today. People try to escape pain in alcohol and drugs, and even in seeking their own deaths as the growing euthanasia movement tells us. Suffering is seen as a great evil, something we are sentenced to endure because of our physical imperfections. But is suffering an evil? I think not for Jesus could not embrace evil, and He embraced suffering. He told His disciples, "Take up your cross and follow Me." All of us will have crosses in life and we can either refuse to lift them or we can accept them in the spirit of the Master.

The great tragedy is not in that people suffer but that, for most, suffering is meaningless. The saints did not hold this latter view but went out of the way to suffer, adopting fasts, scourgings, and other severe penances in order that they might more closely imitate Jesus. They saw suffering not something to be escaped from but to be sought in imitation to Jesus. To them suffering is a shortcut to heaven, a joining with Jesus in His redemptive passion. St. Paul who had a grievous affliction was told by Jesus "my grace is sufficient for you, for my power is made perfect in weakness." As a result Paul joined his sufferings to those of Christ so that "in my flesh I complete what is lacking in Christ's afflictions for the sake of his body, that is, the Church" (Col 1:24).

For the worldly, suffering is meaningless, and so they seek to escape it, but flight was not the choice of Paul and the saints who gave meaning to suffering: It became a way to be more closely united to Christ and a source for merit that they could offer to God on behalf of others in need. Thus suffering, a consequence of original sin, became a participation in the saving work of Jesus. Suffering was not only willingly borne but something sought after. The sadness is not that people suffer but that they do not use their suffering for their own sanctification and the sanctification of others. But this requires faith and faith is greatly lacking in the world.

The Effects of the Sacrament of Anointing of the Sick (C 1520, 1523)

The gift of the Holy Spirit. Through the Holy Spirit the sacrament gives peace, strength, and courage to bear the illness or frailty of age. Trust in God is made stronger so that one can resist the temptations of Satan to discouragement and anguish in the proximity of death. Peace is given in the knowledge that one's sins have been forgiven (Jas 5:15). While the primary purpose is healing of the soul, there can also be healing of the body if such is God's will.

Union with the passion of Christ, as a means of strength and sanctification. This has already been treated above.

Ecclesial grace. Through the doctrines of the Mystical Body and the Communion of Saints, the ill person is united with the whole Church and in bearing pain contributes to the welfare of all the people of God, who in turn intercede for the sick person.

Preparation for the final journey. Just as baptism began our conformity to the death and resurrection of the Lord, this sacrament completes the journey. It is the preparation for those passing on to eternal life. As the Catechism tells us, "This last anointing fortifies the end of our earthly life like a solid rampart for the final struggles before entering the Father's house" (C 1523).

Viaticum. The word "viaticum" is from the Latin meaning "food for the journey," and refers to Holy Communion. While the sacrament of the anointing of the sick can be given to those not in immediate danger of death, it is also given to those whose death is immediate. When this latter is done, viaticum is added by giving the person Holy Communion. As Jesus promised (Jn 6:54), "Those who eat my flesh and drink my blood have eternal life, and I will raise them up on the last day." Thus the reception of the eucharistic sacrament is the final preparation for departing this life.

Viaticum can also be given when a person is in good health but entering a dangerous circumstance, such as a soldier going into battle, a person about to undergo a serious operation, or any occasion when death is highly possible. It is the role of the Church to prepare all of its children to complete their earthly journey in close union with Christ (C 1525).

Summary. The sacraments of baptism, Eucharist, and confirmation are known as sacraments of initiation into Christian life. The sacraments of penance and anointing of the sick are sacraments that complete the Christian life. In addition, there are two other sacraments, marriage and holy orders, that refer to vocation in life. Thus the sacraments of the Church span the whole of life from birth to death.

Review Questions

Show that Jesus established the sacrament of the anointing of the sick.
Must one be in danger of death to receive this sacrament?
Is suffering an evil? Explain your answer.
How does anointing of the sick differ from viaticum?

VI. The Sacrament of Matrimony

The Church's canon law 1055 states: "The matrimonial covenant, by which a man and a woman establish between themselves a partnership of the whole of life, is by its nature ordered towards the good of spouses and the procreation and education of offspring; this covenant between baptized persons has been raised by Christ the Lord to the dignity of a sacrament."

God in sharing His creative power with humans ordained that the family — father, mother, children — was to be the basic unit of society. Thus God is the author of marriage. In the family husband and wife share in God's creative power and share in the spiritual love which God wills. It is reprehensible that today's pagan world has distorted the word "love," which is another name for God (1 Jn 4:16), into a synonym for a sexual act that may be far removed from true spiritual love. Hence, the Church's view of marriage as a sacrament is more important than ever in a society where basic values are under attack.

The Catechism (1603) tells us that "The vocation to marriage is written in the very nature of man and woman as they came from the hand of the Creator." A sense of matrimonial union is found in all cultures and the well-being of human society is closely bound up with the well-being of conjugal and family life. We have earlier shown how God created the world and peopled it out of love. The Bible tells us, "Male and female he created them. God blessed them, and God said to them. 'Be fruitful and multiply, and fill the earth and subdue it' " (Gn 1:27-28). Husband and wife were to be two in one flesh (Mt 19:6). The unity that God willed was weakened by sin as we see from the very beginning in the recriminations of Adam and Eve (Gn 3:9-13). "Nevertheless," the Catechism concludes (1608), "the order of creation persists, though seriously disturbed. To heal the wounds of sin, man and woman need the help of grace that God in his infinite mercy never refuses them. Without his help man and woman cannot achieve the union of their lives for which God created them. . . ." As a source for this needed grace Jesus raised marriage to the rank of a sacrament.

Marriage in the New Law. The first public act of Jesus was at Cana (Jn 2:1-11) when he blessed a marriage with His presence. In His preaching and in His dialogue with the Jewish religious establishment, He spoke of the unity of marriage, "two in one flesh," and its indissolubility, "What God has joined together, let no one separate" (Mk 10:9). Explaining this teaching to His Apostles, He told them (Mk 10:11), "Whoever divorces his wife and marries another commits adultery against her; and if she divorces her husband and marries another, she commits adultery." It is because of this teaching of the Lord that the Catholic Church does not recognize or permit divorce, while it would seem many other Christian churches do not accept the literalness of the command of Christ. That there are Catholics who fail to follow the teaching of the Church and opt for civil divorce is to be regretted. If they attempt a new union, it cannot be recognized as valid (C 1650) and they are separated from eucharistic communion as long as the state exists.

The teaching of Jesus went counter to the culture of His time, just as the teaching of the Church is counter to current custom. St. Paul had to instruct his converts in the apostolic teaching on marriage to counter pagan debauchery. Paul in Ephesians 5 likens the union of marriage to the union of Christ and His Church. Here and in 1 Corinthians 7 he gives lengthy expositions on marriage.

The Celebration of Marriage. In the Latin rite marriage is the only sacrament in which the ordinary ministers are the laity — the bride and groom themselves who are being married. In the Eastern rites it is the priest who is minister of the sacrament, who after an exchange of vows "crowns" the bride and groom. The matter of the sacrament is the marriage contract and the form is the free acceptance ("I do") by the bride and groom. "Free" means that neither party is under any constraint or coercion by external fear to marry and are not impeded by any natural or ecclesiastical law. If freedom is lacking, the marriage is invalid and the marriage later can be annulled by a competent ecclesiastical court as having never taken place.

The marriage takes place before a priest or deacon who witnesses the exchange of vows in the name of the Church and confers the Church's blessing. Normally the marriage takes place during Mass so that the bride and groom unite their own lives with that of Christ in the Eucharist by which they form one body with Christ and themselves. Through the sacrament they receive the Holy Spirit who "is the seal of their covenant, the ever-available source of their love and the strength to renew their fidelity" (C 1624).

Vatican II's Pastoral Constitution on the Church in the Modern World has a whole chapter devoted to marriage that begins by examining the problems facing Christian marriage today, particularly in North America and Europe: the plague of divorce, so-called free love, unmarried mothers, living together outside matrimony. Even marriage itself is often dishonored by selfishness, hedonism, and unlawful contraceptive practices. Add to these the economic, psychological, social, and civil climate, and one can understand that in many places marriage is in crisis.

To counter these circumstances canon law 1063 requires pastors to offer personal preparation for those about to enter marriage so that they understand the nature of Christian marriage and the duties of spouses and parents. After the marriage, the pastor is to provide assistance for maintaining and protecting the conjugal covenant so that husband and wife can lead holier and fuller lives within their families.

The same pastoral constitution reminds it readers, "By its very nature the institution of marriage and married love is ordered to the procreation and education of the offspring and it is in them that it finds its glory." In this aspect of marriage the couple are cooperating with God the Creator. For just reasons spouses may space their children as long as they do nothing artificial to prevent births. As the Catechism (2370) teaches: "Periodic continence, that is, the methods of birth regulation based on self-observation and the use of infertile periods, is in conformity with the objective criteria of morality." This system, known as Natural Family Planning, is very effective in spacing births but it should not be attempted without prior and proper training of husband and wife.

Sins Against Marriage. *Adultery*, or marriage infidelity, takes place when two people, of whom at least one is married, have sexual relations. This is a serious sin of injustice that injures the marriage bond, transgresses the rights of the other spouse, and undermines marriage by breaking the marriage contract. Jesus felt so strongly about this that He even condemned the mere desire, knowing that from desire the action flows. "You have heard that it was said, 'You shall not commit adultery.' But I say to you that everyone who looks at a woman with lust has already committed adultery with her in his heart" (Mt 5:27).

Divorce is a grave offense against the natural law, because it breaks a contract to which the spouses freely assented, to live with each other until death. Divorce introduces disorder into both the family and society. The Church does recognize that there are instances where living together becomes practically impossible and in such a case allows physical separation, and even civil divorce to protect legal rights. But in such a case, the Church still regards the couple as husband and wife and their marriage bond indissoluble.

Free union. This is when a man and woman decline to give juridical and public form to a liaison involving sexual intimacy. Whether this is considered a trial marriage or the inability to make a permanent commitment, it offends against the dignity of marriage and God's moral law. The sexual act is to be exercised only in marriage, and when done outside of marriage is grave sin. For a person to take sacramental Communion in such a state would involve a further sin of sacrilege, which in itself takes on added gravity because it is committed against the Eucharist.

The Domestic Church. Jesus chose to grow up in a human family and thus ennobled all families. Because of attacks on the family today, Vatican II called the family *Ecclesia domestica*, the Domestic Church. The home is the first school of Christian life in which the children are instructed by the word and example of parents who can never be replaced as primary teachers of their children. Every Christian family is expected to be a holy family.

Virginity and Celibacy

Virginity and celibacy are a proper role for a Christian when lived in imitation of Jesus. Jesus held this vocation to be a counsel which some could follow. One day after speaking on divorce His disciples asked Him if it was better not to marry. Jesus gave this answer (Mt 19:12):

"There are eunuchs who have been so from birth, and there are eunuchs who have been made eunuchs by others, and there are eunuchs who have made themselves eunuchs for the sake of the kingdom of heaven. Let anyone accept this who can."

St. Paul chose for himself a life of celibacy and recommended it to his converts but recognized it was not for everyone when he wrote (1 Cor 7:8-9): "To the unmarried and the widows I say that it is well for them to remain unmarried as I am. But if they are not practicing self-control, they should marry. For it is better to marry than to be aflame with passion."

Virginity is a state of life to which all are called before marriage and it is a lifelong vocation for some. It would be wrong to conclude that virginity is greater than marriage or marriage greater than virginity. "Both the sacrament of Matrimony and virginity for the Kingdom of God come from the Lord himself. It is he who gives them meaning and grants them the grace which is indispensable for living them out in conformity with his will" (C 1620). It was God who ordained marriage (Gn 2:24) and the Son of God who invited some to virginity — two vocations, each a path to salvation.

VII. Sacrament of Holy Orders

"Holy Orders is the sacrament through which the mission entrusted by Christ to his apostles continues to be exercised in the Church until the end of time; thus it is a sacrament of apostolic ministry. It includes three degrees: episcopate, presbyterate and diaconate" (C 1536). Although there are three degrees, there is only one sacrament which gives an indelible character to the soul. The minister of the sacrament is a bishop. Jesus Christ is the source of ministry in the Church and this has already been discussed in treating the hierarchical nature of the Church. The matter of the sacrament is the imposition of hands and the form the words used by the ordaining bishop.

The priesthood of the Church was prefigured in the Aaronic priesthood of the Old Testament which came to fulfillment in Christ, the "one mediator between God and men" (1 Tm 2:5), and it is to Christ that the priests of the New Covenant are ministers without diminishing the uniqueness of Christ's priesthood. The priest is ordained to act *in persona*

Christi (in the person of Christ), and this leads to another title for the priest, *alter Christus* (another Christ).

Strangely, some non-Catholics argue that Jesus never established a priesthood while not questioning the right of their own ministers to serve them. There is no denying the fact that Jesus did choose assistants (Mk 3:14) to share in His mission. After His resurrection Jesus reconfirmed this special calling to preach, baptize, and forgive sins (Jn 20:22-23, Mt 28:19-20). Jesus also gave the Apostles power to expand the Church and appoint other assistants, thus their first appointment (Acts 1:26) was to name a successor to Judas. Later as the work grew they appointed seven deacons (Acts 6:6).

In Acts 13:3 Paul and Barnabas are ordained and are sent forth as missioners. Paul in turn ordained Timothy (2 Tm 1:6). Those being ordained were not only bishops to lead but also priests to serve the new Christian communities as Paul instructs Titus to do in Crete (Ti 1:5). Perhaps the difficulty arises because of the use of the Greek word *presbyter*, which translates as priest, or as some use it, elder. In writing to Timothy Paul makes a distinction between a bishop and priest (elder).

Thus in the very early apostolic Church the three degrees of holy orders — bishop, priest, deacon — were already present. The first two are ministerial participation in the priesthood of Christ, and the third a vocation of service to the first two.

Bishops are successors of the Apostles and are ordained to sanctify, rule, and teach. By their appointment they reach the fullness of the sacrament of holy orders. "As Christ's vicar, each bishop has the pastoral care of the particular Church entrusted to him, but at the same time he bears collegially with all his brothers in the episcopacy the solicitude for all the Churches: 'Though each bishop is the lawful pastor only of the portion of the flock entrusted to his care, as a legitimate successor of the apostles he is, by divine institution and precept, responsible with the other bishops for the apostolic mission of the Church' " (interior quotation from Pius XII, *Fidei donum*).

Priests are co-workers of the bishops in the apostolic mission, depending upon their bishop or religious superior for their own proper power. It is in the eucharistic assembly that they exercise in a supreme degree their priestly office. Priests are bound together in a sacramental brotherhood which "finds liturgical expression in the custom of presbyters imposing hands, after the bishop, during the rite of ordination" (C 1568). Priests, like bishops, must be celibates.

Deacons are ordained into a ministry of service. While the Churches of the East have always maintained this order, in the West it was allowed to go into disuse until it was restored by Vatican Council II. Unlike the priesthood, only the bishop lays hands on the deacon at ordination, signifying a special attachment to the bishop in his ministry. The deacon assists in the divine mysteries, in the distribution of Holy Communion, blessing marriages, in the proclamation of the Gospel, preaching, presiding over funerals, and in various ministries of charity.

Only a baptized male can be called to holy orders. The Lord chose only men for His apostolic college and the Church cannot do otherwise. No one has the right to ordination; it is a call from God, signified in the call by the bishop or superior.

Review Questions

What is the purpose of marriage?
Who is the author of marriage? Explain your answer.
Who is the minister of the sacrament of matrimony?
What is the difference between divorce and annulment?
Is marriage preferable to virginity or vice versa?
What are the three grades of holy orders?
What are the three roles of the bishop?
Where does the priest exercise his office in the supreme
    degree?

10. The Commandments of God

One day a well-to-do young man approached Jesus and asked Him, "Rabbi, what must I do to have eternal life?" Jesus told him, "If you wish to enter into life, keep the commandments" (cf. Mt 19:16-17). During His Sermon on the Mount, Jesus declared, "Do not think that I have come to abolish the law or the prophets; I have come not to abolish but to fulfill" (Mt 5:17). In the same sermon Jesus expatiated on the commandments, showing that they covered more than the words seem to show. For example, He told the people, "You have heard it was said to those of ancient times, 'You shall not murder'; and, 'whoever murders shall be liable to judgment.' But I say to you that if you are angry with a brother . . , you will be liable to judgment" (Mt 5:21-22). And again (5:27), "You have heard that it was said, 'You shall not commit adultery.' But I say to you that everyone who looks at a woman with lust has already committed adultery with her in his heart." It is important then that we know the fullness of each commandment.

Origin of the Decalogue. The word "Decalogue" literally means "ten words." During the exodus the Jews arrived at Mount Sinai and Moses went to the top to pray to God. God spoke to Moses telling him that the Jews would be His treasured possession out of all the peoples and that on the third day God would reveal to Moses what the Jews would have to do for their part in the covenant. On the third day Moses again went up Sinai in a great storm of thunder and lightning. Out of the tempest God spoke His Ten Commandments which were to be observed (Ex 20:1-17 and Deut 5:1-21).

These commandments can be summarized into two categories: the first three that concern relationship with God and the last seven relationship with other people. Jesus made this division in answering a lawyer's question about which was the greatest commandment (Mt 22:34-40). Jesus replied,

" 'You shall love the Lord your God with all your heart, and with all your soul, and with all your mind.' This is the greatest and first commandment. And the second is like it: 'You shall love your neighbor like yourself.' On these two commandments hang all the law and the prophets."

There is a reciprocal unity to the Decalogue (C 2069). "To transgress one commandment is to infringe all the others." As St. James tells us (Jas 2:10), whoever fails in one point "has become accountable for all of it." In offending our neighbor, we offend God his creator. In offending God, one offends the unity of the Mystical Body.

Obligation of the Decalogue (C 2072). Because the Decalogue is the word of God, the obligation to obey it is a *grave* obligation. God does not speak to us in vain. The obligation to obey the commandments binds at all times and in every place. Because the commandments are God's laws, no power on earth can dispense from them.

The Catechism says, "The Ten Commandments are engraved by God in the human heart." Vatican Council II (*Gaudium et Spes*, 16) puts it more directly: "Deep within his conscience man discovers a law which he has not laid upon himself but which he must obey. . . . For man has in his heart a law inscribed by God. . . . His conscience is man's most secret core, and his sanctuary."

Conscience

"Conscience is a judgment of reason whereby the human person recognizes the moral quality of a concrete act that he is going to perform, is in the process of performing, or has already completed" (C 1778). It is the prudent judgment of conscience that leads us to obey the laws of God. Vatican II in its *Declaration on Religious Liberty* states that "(Man) must not be forced to act contrary to his conscience. Nor must he be prevented from acting according to his conscience, especially in religious matters."

The formation of conscience is a lifelong task. Children have to be trained to do what is moral and right, and adults must ponder the laws of God and the Church so that an erroneous judgment is avoided. It is a basic rule that one can never do evil so that good results from it, no matter how great and important that good may seem. The end does not justify the means. It is possible for conscience to make an erroneous judgment, brought about by failure to seek the truth or brought about "when conscience is by degrees almost blinded through the habit of committing sin. In such a case the person is culpable. Errors in judgment can be caused by ignorance of the Gospel, the bad example of others, enslavement to one's passions, rejection of the Church's authority and teaching, a mistaken notion of the autonomy of conscience. Conscience is to be judged against objective standards and not subjective preferences.

I. The First Commandment

I am the LORD your God, who brought you out of the land of Egypt, out of the house of slavery; you shall have no other gods before me. You shall not make for yourself an idol. . . . You shall not bow down to them or worship them. . . .

Deut 5:6-9

God makes His commandments known to the Israelites by first reminding them that He is their liberator and the only one and true God. In revealing Himself as LORD, He is telling us that we must have faith in Him and acknowledge His authority. In our relationship with God, we are bound by faith, hope, and charity.

Faith. St. Paul tells us that our relationship with God should be one of "obedience of faith" (Rom 16:26). "Our duty toward God is to believe in him and bear witness to him" (C 2087). Thus we must protect our faith and make it grow and avoid everything that would lessen faith. Sins against faith include: *voluntary doubt* which refuses to hold true what God has revealed to us and which the Church proposes for belief; *incredulity* (unbelief), which is the neglect of revealed truth or the willful refusal to assent to it; *schism,* which is the separation from the unity of the Church, from communion with the members of the Church, from the jurisdiction of the pope; *heresy,* which is the obstinate post-baptismal denial of some truth that must be believed in faith; *apostasy*, which is total repudiation of the Catholic faith.

Hope. Hope is a virtue that makes us desire life with God and gives us the confidence that we will receive the necessary grace to accomplish this end. Sins against hope are: *despair*, which is a willful and complete abandonment of hope, and this is contrary to God's goodness, justice, and mercy; *presumption*, which is overconfidence in one's own abilities to attain salvation or expecting salvation without conversion or merit (e.g., "God sends no one to hell").

Charity. God's love for us asks us to respond in kind. We are to love God above all else and to love His creation. We can sin against God's love by *indifference*, *ingratitude*, *lukewarmness*, *spiritual sloth*, or *hatred of God*.

What We Owe God

The theological virtues of faith, hope, and charity cause us to ponder what we as creatures owe to our Creator in justice. This attitude of creature to creator is called the *virtue of religion*. This virtue disposes us to adoration, prayer, sacrifice, promises, and vows.

Adoration, the first act of the virtue of religion, is that supreme honor that is due only to God, who is our Creator and Savior, our Lord and Master. We acknowledge our nothingness and total dependence on God. We praise and extol Him. Mary's Magnificat (Lk 1:46-55) is an excellent example of a prayer of adoration. Worship of God in the three Persons of the Trinity should be part of our daily prayer. Adoration must be distinguished from *veneration*, which is that respect we give to God's saints because of the holiness of their lives.

Prayer is the lifting up of the mind to God. It is enjoined by the First Commandment. For many people prayer is mainly the prayer of petition; they pray to God when they are in need or hurting. Prayer to God, however, is far broader. We can learn to pray properly by remembering the word ARTS. We begin prayer in *adoration* of God, acknowledging Him as our creator who loves and cares for us; we praise God for simply being who He is. This is followed by *reparation* in which we ask God's forgiveness for our offenses against Him, recognizing that we do not serve Him as well as we should. Then our prayer turns to *thanksgiving* for all that He has given us. Only after these devotions does our prayer become one of *supplication* in which we present our petitions and needs.

How often should we pray? Jesus told us "to pray always and not to lose heart" (Lk 18:1). Paul gave the same advice to his converts, telling them to "pray without ceasing" (1 Thes 5:17). At first glance this advice may seem impossible to us but following it is very simple. If upon rising each morning, we offer all we do that day to God, then this morning offering makes everything we do that day a prayer whether it be the work of our job, cleaning the house, driving to market, or even our recreation. Of course there should also be formal prayer — morning prayer, evening prayer, private devotions, Mass, and Holy Communion, and for those systematically working toward perfection such things as meditation and noon particular examen (self-examination regarding growth in virtue).

Sacrifice. This is offering something of value to God in homage or propitiation. The Old Testament gives many examples of sacrifice from Abraham's readiness to sacrifice his son Isaac to the Temple sacrifices offered in the time of Jesus. In the New Testament we are given the only perfect sacrifice of Jesus being offered on the Cross "as a total offering to the Father's love and for our salvation" (C 2100). Each time we take part in the Mass, we join ourselves to this sacrifice of Jesus. We can also offer God sacrifices of our own, particularly in the penitential times of Lent and Advent.

Promises and *vows.* We make formal promises to God in receiving the sacraments of baptism, confirmation, matrimony, and holy orders. We can also make informal promises to God to do some action or charity, such as almsgiving, making a pilgrimage, performing a certain devotion, etc. Because God is faithful to us, we must be faithful to God. Hence one should not make promises to God without careful consideration of all that is involved and preferably after consulting a confessor or spiritual director.

Canon law 1191 defines a vow this way: "A vow is a deliberate and free promise made to God concerning a possible and better good which must be fulfilled by reason of the virtue of religion." By its very nature a vow sets up a grave obligation for fulfillment but can be dispensed for a just reason by the local ordinary or a pastor. Because of the grave nature of a vow it should never be made on the spur of the moment but only after serious study and permission of one's confessor or spiritual director. Rash vows should never be made.

You Shall Have No Other Gods Before Me

"The first commandment forbids honoring gods other than the one Lord who has revealed himself to his people. It proscribes superstition and irreligion. Superstition in some sense represents a perverse excess of religion; irreligion is the vice contrary by defect to the virtue of religion" (C 2110).

Superstition. This is a belief that some action or circumstance not logically related to the course of events influences its outcome (cf. *American Heritage Dictionary*). Superstition gives false or unworthy worship to God, or divine worship to a creature. Examples of excesses in religion are false or exaggerated devotions, chain letters or prayers, believing some favor must be published as a condition for it to be granted, unfailing prayers. Superstitions of irreligion are such things as magic, fortune telling, giving power to crystals, reincarnation, necromancy (calling up spirits of the dead), divination, foretelling future events by augury, vain observances such as bad luck from a black cat or good luck from a rabbit's foot, or idolatry.

Idolatry (from the Greek *eidololatreia*, image worship). Idolatry is worship given to some person or thing. The Old Testament gives many examples of idolatry among the tribes that surrounded the Israelites. God sent prophets to condemn these idols when their images were imported into Israel. The psalmist (115:3-5) praises true worship ("Our God is in the heavens") with pagan belief ("Their idols are silver and gold, the work of human hands. They have mouths but do not speak; eyes, but do not see.") Many of the early Christians were put to death for not adoring the pagan gods of Rome.

Idolatry, however, goes beyond the images of false idols. Many people create the false gods of money, power, pleasure, race, beauty, luxury, the State (as in Communist Russia or Nazi Germany). Elements of the New Age which worships Native American gods or wicca (witches worshiping spirits of nature) are forms of idolatry. A virulent and deadly form of idolatry is satanism. All these are a perversion of our inborn sense of religion (St. Augustine recognized this when he wrote: "Our hearts are restless until they find rest in Thee").

Irreligion. A biblical example of irreligion is Satan's temptation of Jesus in the desert which Jesus recognized as irreligion by quoting Deuteronomy to the tempter, "Do not put the Lord your God to the test" (Mt 4:7, Deut 6:16). Thus Jesus revealed that *tempting God* is a grave sin. *Sacrilege* is also a grave sin of irreligion. Sacrilege consists in profaning or treating unworthily the sacraments and other liturgical actions, as well as persons, things, or places consecrated to God. Violation or unworthy reception of the Eucharist is a particularly grave form of sacrilege because it is an offense against the true body of Christ made substantially present. Another sin of irreligion is that of *simony*. This sin is named after Simon the magician (Acts 8:9-24) who sought to buy the power of the Apostles from Peter. The sin is the willful attempt to buy or sell something spiritual or something material connected with the spiritual, e.g., buying or selling absolution, the administration of a sacrament, relics, indulgences, etc.

You Shall Not Make for Yourself a Graven Image

This part of the commandment refers to idols. It must be remembered that the Jewish people were surrounded by pagans who worshipped their graven images (idols). God wanted the Jews to keep themselves free of these foreign influences. A good example of failure in this regard is in the story of King Solomon, who began his reign faithful to the Lord, building the first great Temple. But as Solomon married foreign wives, they brought their idols into his kingdom. God became angry at Solomon (1 Kgs 11:9) for failing in this commandment and foretold that Solomon's heir would lose the kingdom as punishment.

The biblical distinction between images and idols is quite clear. Moses was not condemned for the image of the brazen serpent. Solomon was not condemned for the images of angels and animals that he had sculpted in his Temple and palace but for the idols imported by his foreign wives which led Israelites astray.

Some enemies of the Catholic Church condemn the Church for using statues, icons, and other paintings in the decoration of its churches. Such decoration has been around since apostolic Christianity as the Roman catacombs show. The Church uses these images as visual aids for the faith of its people. Catholics do not worship these images, as is sometimes claimed, but they do give them respect for what they represent. Each year many thousands of people visit the Lincoln Memorial in Washington. They go there, not to worship the heroic statue of Abraham Lincoln, but to pay honor to the memory of a great president. It is the same in St. Peter's Basilica in Rome. Thousands each year visit the Pieta, Michelangelo's masterpiece, not to worship a piece of marble but to honor and pray to those whom the statue represents, the crucified Jesus and His Mother.

That some abuses can exist is not to be denied. Uneducated people can become superstitious, using medals or other objects as charms and amulets, attaching power to them that they do not have. Such practices are condemned by the Church as a violation of the First Commandment. Some people can also mix true religion with pagan practices as we find in voodoo or Santeria, but again this is condemned by the Church. Superstition, which often has an element of fear connected with it, is difficult to destroy without education.

The Catechism (2132) sums it up, "The honor paid to

sacred images is a 'respectful veneration,' not the adoration due God alone."

II. The Second Commandment

You shall not make wrongful use of the name of the LORD your God.

Ex 20:7

The second commandment tells us that the name of God is holy and must be treated with respect as demanded by the virtue of religion. In the old Jewish culture a person was not known until his or her name was known. That is why Moses asked God for His name. God replied that His name was Yahweh ("I am who am"). This name was so sacred that the Jews refused to speak it and when it was written, only the consonants (YHWH) were used. In its place they used El, a name for God in Semitic languages, and Adonai (Lord). Even today strict Jews will not write the word God but print it G-d. Respect for God's name is indicative of the respect we must have for God Himself and the whole of sacred reality. Thus this commandment demands respect in speech and writing not only for God but also for those persons and things that are close to God.

We abuse the name of God by every improper use of the names of God, the Father, Jesus Christ, the Holy Spirit, the Blessed Virgin, and the saints. We take the name of the Lord in vain when we use it without the respect it demands or in something trivial. We must venerate God's name and be always aware that its misuse offends divinity. There are various ways that we sin against the second commandment.

Blasphemy is committed by speaking against God (inwardly or outwardly) words of hatred, reproach, or defiance.

Promises made in the name of God must be kept and should not be made lightly since they involve God's truthfulness and authority which is called upon as witness.

Oaths, or what are popularly known as swearing and cursing, are to be avoided because they involve God in something trivial or wrong and show an irreverence for God's majesty and power. For a good and serious purpose one may call upon God as a witness as Paul does in Second Corinthians 1:23 when he calls God as witness to the truth of what he is saying, and again in Galatians 1:20 when he writes, "before God, I do not lie."

Legal oaths. The Church recognizes the right of lawful authority to demand an oath for a grave and just reason as giving gravity and solemnity to what is being pledged. This type of oath is a solemn promise to tell the truth, made in the name of One who is Truth itself. To take a false oath in this respect is the sin of *perjury*, which is committed when one makes a promise under oath with no intention of keeping it, or when after promising one does not keep the promise.

Evil oaths. One can never take an oath to do evil and this kind of an oath is never binding. Such an oath is a mockery of the divine name. These oaths are sometimes found in secret societies which pledge a recruit to illegal wrongdoings.

III. The Third Commandment

Remember the sabbath day, and keep it holy. Six days shall you labor and do all your work. But the seventh day is a sabbath to the LORD your God; you shall not do any work.

Ex 20:8-10

The third commandment ordains that the sabbath be kept holy and not be profaned by unnecessary human labor. It is a day to be set aside to the Lord. Jewish law surrounded the sabbath with many restrictions, even to the doing of good. Jesus used the sabbath as a holy day and often used it as an occasion of teaching (Mk 1:21). Nevertheless He was critical of some of the legalistic restrictions imposed on the Jewish people by their religious leaders, reminding them that "The sabbath was made for man, not man for the sabbath" (Mk 2:27), concluding "the Son of man is lord even of the sabbath."

The very early Church was almost totally Jewish. Those Christians worshiped in Temple and synagogues on the sabbath and then came together on the evening of the first day of the week where "They devoted themselves to the apostles' teaching and fellowship, to the breaking of bread (Eucharist) and the prayers" (Acts 2:42). But as the Church spread beyond the Holy Land and more and more gentiles entered it, knowing little or nothing of the Jewish sabbath, they accepted without question the Apostles' decision that for Christians the day of ceremonial worship would be the first day of the week.

The first day of the week (Sunday) is the day when God began creation of the world in a formless void and commanded "there be light" (Gn 1:1-3), but even more important for Christians it is the day when Christ arose from the dead and the new creation began. It was to be "the first of all days, the first of all feasts, the Lord's Day — Sunday" (C 2174). The right of Peter and the Apostles to make this decision was given by Jesus in granting the power of the keys (Mt 16:19). It was the New Law replacing the Old. Sunday worship fulfills the moral command to set aside a day of rest on which God is particularly honored. St. Ignatius of Antioch, one of the Fathers of the Church, who was martyred c. 107, put it this way: "Those who lived according to the old order of things have come to a new hope, no longer keeping the sabbath, but the Lord's Day, in which our life is blessed by Him and by His death."

Obligation of the Sunday

The Sunday celebration is thus governed by the third commandment and the law of the Church. Canon 1246 states: "Sunday is the day on which the paschal mystery is celebrated in light of the apostolic tradition and is to be observed as the foremost holy day of obligation in the universal Church." The canon goes on to add other holy days of obligation: Nativity of Jesus, Epiphany, Ascension of Christ, Body and Blood of Christ, Mary the Mother of God, Immaculate Conception, the Assumption, St. Joseph, Sts. Peter and Paul, and All Saints. The canon adds that national conferences of bishops can transfer these latter feasts to a Sunday or drop them altogether with approval from the Holy See.

Catholics are bound in conscience to participate in Mass on all Sundays and prescribed holy days (canon 1247). The

Sunday Eucharist is central to Catholic life. It is not only a communal celebration of the Church but it is testimony of one's faith in Christ and in the Church. Those who deliberately fail in keeping this commandment of God and the Church without a justifying cause (e.g., illness, unavoidable travel, lack of transportation to a distant church, etc.) are guilty of grave (mortal) sin.

IV. The Fourth Commandment

Honor your father and your mother.

Ex 20:12

The first three commandments speak of our relationship with God and the remaining seven of our relationship with our neighbors whom Jesus defined as meaning all people, even enemies (Lk 10:36-37). The bidding of the fourth commandment shows that God wills that after Him we should honor our parents to whom we owe life, and in doing so, God is testing parents with His authority. As the Catechism shows, this commandment goes beyond parents to all in authority: teachers, governors, employers, leaders — their relationship with us, and our relationship with them.

The Family

As discussed under the sacrament of matrimony, God has ordained that marriage exists for the good of spouses and the procreation and education of children. As such the family is the basic social unit and does not depend upon recognition by any political authority, although authority has the duty to protect it and nourish its growth. The Church teaches (Pastoral Constitution on the Church in the Modern World, 52) that civil authority "should consider it a sacred duty to acknowledge the true nature of marriage and the family, to protect and foster them, to safeguard public morality and promote domestic prosperity." Parents are the primary guardians and teachers of their children and the State can take no action that would deny this basic right. Intrusion by the State in parental responsibility was found under Nazism and Communism when the State took complete control of the political and moral education of children; but, this intrusion continues to exist in what are referred to as "democratic" countries where laws permit minor girls to seek abortion without obtaining parental consultation or where public school education advocates immoral sexual practices.

The Christian family is referred to as a little church where moral living is not only taught but also caught in the Christian example of the parents. The Christian family is an image of the communion of Father, Son, and Holy Spirit; it has a model in the Holy Family of Nazareth. The respect of children for their parents is required by this commandment as long as the parents live. While the children dwell within the family unit, they are required to give obedience to their parents as St. Paul instructs: "Children, obey your parents in everything, for this is your acceptable duty in the Lord" (Col 3:20) Paul is not one sided, he instructs parents: "Do not provoke your children to anger, but bring them up in the discipline and instruction of the Lord" (Eph 6:4).

Filial respect requires grown children to recognize responsibilities towards parents, particularly support in old age and in times of illness, loneliness, or distress (C 2218). Filial respect extends to relationships between brothers and sisters. If a bond of charity exists between offspring, imagined or real animosities which divide so many families can be avoided.

When children become adults they have the right "to choose their profession and state of life" (C 2230). It is good for them to seek the advice and counsel of their parents but always the final decision is their own. Parents must be careful not to apply direct or indirect pressure against a child's choice of profession or spouse; there is a distinction between pressure and prudent giving of advice.

Civil Society

The fourth commandment also embraces our relationships within civil society: the duties of those who exercise authority as well as those subject to legitimate civil authority.

All authority comes from God and involves service to those who live under that authority (Mt 12:49). All authority is obliged to respect the fundamental and inalienable rights of the human person and have particular concern for the family and the disadvantaged. The common good of the community is a determining factor in decisions. Care must be taken that personal preferences do not outweigh the common good and the aspirations of the human community.

On the part of citizens submission must be paid to legitimate authority, reserving always the right of balanced protest of actions that are harmful to the good of the community. Speaking of civil authority (Rom 13:7), St. Paul lays down this rule for citizens: "Pay to all what is due them — taxes to whom taxes are due, revenue to whom revenue is due, respect to whom respect is due, honor to whom honor is due" (also see Ti 3:1). Paul is thus telling the Roman Christians that they have the duty to contribute to the good of society. Citizens also have the duty to vote and to defend one's country (C 2240).

The Church has always regarded *patriotism* (the love of one's country) as a virtue akin to justice which requires one to pay debts to one's country and to charity which requires us to love our neighbor. Patriotism must be distinguished from nationalism which is a vice. Nationalism takes on the aspects of a false religion and is thus condemned. It is opposed to the Church's teaching on the unity of the human race and the brotherhood of humanity under the Fatherhood of God. The logical development of nationalism is the omnipotent State in which people exist for the State and not vice versa. In modern times Nazism, Fascism, and Communism arose from this false patriotism.

Review Questions

What is the Decalogue? Give its origin.
What are the two categories of commandments?
What is the First Commandment?
What do we owe God and how do we show it?
How do we sin against the First Commandment?
Distinguish between idols and images.

Does the Catholic use of statues violate this commandment?
How does the Second Commandment differ from the First?
Mention some sins against the Second Commandment.
Why do Catholics commemorate the Sabbath on Sunday?
What is the obligation of the Sunday?
What is the Fourth Commandment?
What does filial respect require?
Why is the family the basic unit of society?
Is the Church the primary teacher of children?
Why should citizens submit to civil authority?
What is the difference between patriotism and nationalism?

V. The Fifth Commandment

You shall not kill.

Ex 20:13

The Congregation for the Doctrine of the Faith, acting under the authority of the pope, declared in its Instruction on The Gift of Life (*Donum vitae*): "Human life is sacred because from its beginning it involves the creative action of God and it remains for ever in a special relationship with the Creator, who is its sole end. God alone is the Lord of life from its beginning until its end: no one can under any circumstance claim for himself the right directly to destroy an innocent human being." The key words in the directive above are "directly" and "innocent."

"To kill a human being, in whom the image of God is present, is a particularly serious sin. Only God is the master of life," Pope John Paul II wrote in his letter The Gospel of Life. "By the authority which Christ conferred on Peter and his successors, and in communion with the bishops of the Catholic Church, I confirm that the direct and voluntary killing of an innocent is always gravely immoral."

Murder appeared at the beginning of human history when Adam's son Cain slew his brother Abel. For his crime Cain was condemned by God and driven into exile. Thus from the very beginning, murder was considered not only a heinous crime but an invasion of God's authority over life and death. Murder is wrong because it is a sin against justice and charity. Murder deprives another of his or her God-given right to life. Murder is a violation of the Golden Rule and the command to love one another.

Legitimate Defense

Individuals as well as nations have the right to resist an unjust aggressor, using means proportionate to the threat. Hence the State or an individual is not guilty of murder if either, in defense of life, is forced into lethal action. Legitimate authority has not only a right but an obligation to protect the rights of individuals as well as the common good of the family and the State. St. Thomas Aquinas in considering this question approached it from the principle of double effect: "The act of self-defense can have a double effect: the preservation of one's own life and the killing of the aggressor. . . . The one is intended, the other is not. As noted above, the means used must be proportionate to the threat. If one can end the threat in a less drastic way (e.g., wounding or causing to flee), then the lesser means should be followed.

Under this principle the State has the right and duty to punish malefactors and, in cases of extreme gravity, even by the death penalty (C 2266). Society has the right to protect itself and those who threaten civil order can be removed from society. In the case of murder, it is preferable to incarcerate the criminal without possibility of parole. Punishment is undertaken to redress the disorder caused by the offense, to preserve public order, and for the safety of citizens.

Abortion

Before I formed you in the womb I knew you,
and before you were born I consecrated you. . . .

Jer 1:5

These words of God which open the Book of the Prophet Jeremiah speak of God as the author of human life and of God's plan for that life when it develops.

The Catechism (2270) tells us: "Human life must be respected and protected absolutely from the moment of conception. From the first moment of his existence, a human being must be recognized as having the rights of a person — among which is the inviolable right of every innocent being to life." Proponents of abortion avoid the question of what kind of life is present after conception, but any biologist can tell them that it is the beginning of human life, programmed for the child and adult it is to become.

While legalized abortion is rampant today, the Church's opposition to this destruction of human life is not something recent but has been a constant teaching since apostolic times. The *Didache* (Teaching of the Twelve Apostles) states the principle clearly: "You shall not kill by abortion or by infanticide." This teaching is also found in the works of Christian writers of the early Church. Up until present times this crime against life was recognized as such and was done in shame and secrecy. Now with the loss of faith and with a growing anti-population and radical feminist movement, which with the paid aid of professional formers of public opinion, using tested slogans such as "freedom of choice" and "a woman's right to her body," legal approval for abortion has been won and is now being exported worldwide.

In Pope John Paul II's encyclical *Evangelium Vitae*, The Gospel of Life, definitive language is used on the condemnation of abortion. The pope writes: "By the authority which Christ conferred upon Peter and his successors, in communion with the bishops, . . I declare that direct abortion, that is, abortion willed as an end or a means, always constitutes a grave moral disorder, since it is the deliberate killing of an innocent human being."

The abortion movement is the heir to the birth control movement promoted by the eugenicist Margaret Sanger (c. 1919) as a means to purify the race by getting rid of the lower classes through birth control methods, then also illegal. Using sloganeering and illegal clinics, the contraception movement grew and expanded beyond the class for which it was originally intended. A suit opposing a Connecticut law against artificial contraception reached the Supreme Court which ruled against Connecticut and made contraception legal throughout the United States. From preventing births to destroying a fetus is a logical step for the anti-population people (Population Council, Planned Parenthood, etc). Following the birth control successful method, abortion was also brought before the Supreme Court and the Roe vs. Wade decision made legalized abortion the law of the land.

Expensive and persuasive propagandizing, coupled with a nelpful media, has concealed the ethical and moral values that are being destroyed. The Catholic Church has stood almost alone in opposing the contraceptive tactics while stressing the morality of God's laws. The Church does have some allies in its opposition to abortion, churches and people who intuitively sense that immorality has gone too far. But, until people realize that artificial birth control and abortion are close cousins and that morality is a seamless garment, the inroads against life for eugenic reasons will continue to flourish and expand.

Euthanasia

The next logical step in the war against unwanted human life is euthanasia, through which handicapped, sick, and suffering people are to be persuaded to seek death. Again the propaganda slogans ("death with dignity" and "right to die") are being loudly announced and public opinion is being changed. If past pattern is followed, a well-funded case will go before a state court and then the Supreme Court, whose past decisions foretell yet another conclusion against basic natural law. When that day arrives, the only place left to go is in the Nazi pattern when the State will decide who will live and whose "unproductive" life is expendable.

Again the Church is almost a lone voice in teaching that euthanasia is morally unacceptable. It is the Church which proclaims that it is the State's and society's obligation to aid the sick and handicapped to lead lives as normal as possible. It is the Church which urges the sick to find a spiritual meaning in suffering as a way to closer union with God. It is the Church which tells us that all life has meaning and is never useless. It is the Church which insists that God alone is the author of life and master of death, and that we are but stewards and caretakers of the life God gives us.

Speaking about euthanasia in the encyclical The Gospel of Life, Pope John Paul II declared, "In harmony with the magisterium of my predecessors and in communion with the bishops of the Catholic Church, I confirm that euthanasia is a grave violation of the law of God, since it is the deliberate and morally unacceptable killing of a human person. . . . Abortion and euthanasia are thus crimes which no human law can claim to legitimize. . . . There is a grave and clear obligation to oppose them by conscientious objection."

Suicide

Suicide, the taking of one's own life, is a grave offense to the will of God. God has placed within us a natural instinct for the preservation and perpetuation of life. As explained above, we are only stewards of the life God has given us, and it is not a right for us to dispose of it. Suicide also offends the love we are to have for our neighbor because it breaks family ties and is contrary to the love we should have for our Creator.

Suicide very often takes place under a clouded mind. The Catechism (2282) tells us, "Grave psychological disturbances, anguish, or grave fear of hardship, suffering, or torture can diminish the responsibility of the one committing suicide." Because of doubts about the mental state of a suicide, the Church, unless contrary evidence is present, allows Christian burial.

Jesus, early in the Sermon on the Mount (Mt 5:21-22), broadens the Fifth Commandment by adding sins of anger, hatred, and vengeance. The Church adds such sins as scandal which can cause the spiritual death of another. Jesus angrily condemned the scandal given by some of the Jewish religious leaders (Mt 7:15), referring to them as "wolves in sheep's clothing." On another occasion (Mt 18:6) Jesus warned leaders, who gave scandal to followers, telling them, "It would be better for you if a great millstone were fastened around your neck and you were drowned in the depth of the sea." St. Paul was very conscious of his conduct and refused to eat meat lest he give scandal (1 Cor 8:13) to his converts.

The Church also reminds us that this commandment requires that we must take care of our health, not to put our safety at serious risk to practice temperance in the use of food, alcohol, tobacco, medicine — things that are not wrong in themselves when used in moderation but become wrong by abuse. In short, anything that violates bodily integrity is opposed to the Fifth Commandment. Finally, the whole subject of war and peace must be judged in the light of this commandment.

Review Questions

What is the Fifth Commandment?
Why is human life sacred?
Explain the teaching on unjust aggression.
Why is abortion always wrong?
How did the contraception movement develop?
What is the Church's teaching on artificial contraception?
What is the next logical step after abortion?
Why does the Church ordinarily allow Christian burial of a
    suicide?
Name some other sins against the Fifth Commandment.
What does the Fifth Commandment oblige positively?

VI. The Sixth Commandment

You shall not commit adultery.

Ex 20:14

The Book of Genesis (5:1-2) tells us, "When God created man, he made him in the likeness of God. Male and female he created them, and he blessed them and named them 'man.' " This passage from Scripture reveals at once the unity and duality of human creation. In creating humans in His likeness, God was also giving them a share in the continuance of His creation, "Be fruitful and multiply" (Gn 1:27). Sexuality was the means ordained by God through which the human race was to be continued. That there was pleasure in it was an encouragement to its use for the end intended by God.

Sexuality was not given as a toy or plaything and its unity symbolized the communion of husband and wife in marriage, the only place sexuality could be legitimately used. When the complementarity and unity of sexuality are distorted, sins against the Sixth Commandment arise.

It follows from the above that all Christians, married and unmarried, are called to a life of *chastity*, a virtue allied to temperance. Chastity means the abstention from all unlawful sexual pleasure of mind or body. For the unmarried every deliberate sexual act is to be avoided. For the married, chastity means a relative restraint in keeping with the marriage vows and right reason: adultery, voyeurism, sex forced on one's partner, and pornography are some violations of chastity.

People who wish to lead a chaste life should be aware of the *psychology of sin*. All sin begins first in the intellect and is judged there; it is then passed on to the will and finally into action. The longer sin is considered in the intellect, the more difficult is it for the will to refuse consent. Jesus, who was a master of human psychology, knew this and that is why He declared: "You have heard that it was said, 'You shall not commit adultery.' But I say to you that every one who looks at a woman lustfully has already committed adultery with her in his heart." In saying this, Jesus equated the gravity of mental sins with sins of actual commission. Temptations against chastity will arise from our imperfect nature; as soon as they are recognized, they should be dismissed at once from the intellect and not be presented to the will. Self-mastery grows from constant practice.

Christians striving to live a life of chastity must maintain custody of eyes and ears. It should be recognized that the world in which we live is not a Christian world but one ruled by pagan values. Secular books, magazines, television, motion pictures, theater are at best amoral with only rare exceptions. The Christian is bombarded on every side with these worldly values which exist apart from moral considerations. Enough temptations will arise from natural concupiscence (C 1264) without inviting them in under the guise of entertainment. Special care should be taken by those engaged to be married, to make the engagement period a time of mutual respect, an apprenticeship in fidelity, the hope of receiving one another from God, and a time for growth in chastity. Virginity is the greatest gift people can bring to each other in marriage.

Sins Against Chastity

Adultery, or marriage infidelity, is committed when a person has sexual relations with one who is not his or her spouse. It is so grave a sin against justice and chastity that Jesus condemned even the thought.

Lust is disordered desire for, or inordinate enjoyment of, sexual pleasure, particularly when isolated from its procreative and unitive purpose. It is called a deadly sin because it leads to other sins and was specifically condemned by Jesus (Mt 5:28).

Masturbation is the deliberate stimulation of the sexual organs in order to derive sexual pleasure. It is a sin because any use of the sexual faculty outside marriage is contrary to its God-given purpose. The Church's *Declaration of Certain Problems in Sexual Ethics* (9) declares that masturbation is "an intrinsically and gravely disordered action" and rejects the claim of modern psychology that it is a natural part of adolescence.

Fornication is carnal union between an unmarried man and a unmarried woman. It is gravely contrary to the dignity of sexuality which is ordered towards the good of spouses and the generation of children.

Pornography is the written, graphic, or other form of communication designed to excite lewd feelings and excite the sexual appetite. There is a whole creative industry today that produces pornographic material that "does grave injury to the dignity of its participants (actors, vendors, the public), since each one becomes an object of base pleasure and illicit profit for others" (C 2354). It is a grave offense against chastity.

Artificial birth control. This has already been referred to under the sacrament of matrimony. It is Church teaching that every marriage act must remain open to life as this is a fundamental purpose of marriage. However, using a woman's natural cycles of fecundity, Catholics may space births. Once the method of Natural Family Planning is learned and followed exactly, it is more effective than most artificial methods, safer for the woman, and does not carry with its use the possibility of being abortive.

There are other sins opposed to chastity. *Prostitution* is a grave sin against chastity and a social scourge. It has the added sin of scandal when it involves children and adolescents. *Rape* is the forcible sexual violation of another person against that person's will. It is not only a sin against chastity but also against justice and charity. *Incest* is the term for intimate relations between relatives or in-laws within a degree that prohibits marriage between them. It is a particularly grave offense because it "corrupts family relationships and marks a regression toward animality" (C 2388). Incest has added gravity when perpetrated by adults on children or adolescents. "*Living together,*" or sometimes misnamed free union or trial marriage, is an arrangement between a man and woman who refuse to give juridical form to a liaison involving sexual intimacy. Since the sexual act outside marriage is a grave sin, living together is a continual state of sin that excludes one from reception of the Eucharist.

Homosexuality

Homosexuality refers to sexual relations between people of the same sex (men or women) who "experience an exclusive or predominant sexual attraction" (C 2357). In today's permissive climate many non-homosexuals look upon homosexual acts with tolerance or excuse them completely. Homosexuals themselves argue that their unalterable condition, which they did not choose, makes it impossible for them to lead solitary lives. Neither attitude is acceptable to the Church; the first ignores the creative purpose of sexuality, and the second is a denial of free will or an unacceptable excuse against trying to live a chaste life.

Homosexuals, like everyone else, are called to live chaste lives and to seek perfection. Homosexuals can learn self-mastery through the support of disinterested friendship, by prayer, and sacramental grace. The Church does offer the assistance of its sacraments and their grace, as well as giving support to organizations such as Courage, but the majority, caught up in an artificial militancy, will not make the attempt.

Homosexual acts are presented by Sacred Scripture as gravely disordered and even portrays them as the tragic consequence of rejecting God (Rom 1:24-25). Homosexual acts are wrong because they sin against the natural law by closing the sexual act to the gift of life. Hence, the Church's position is that they can never be approved in any way and under no circumstances.

Nevertheless, Christians must accept homosexuals with respect, compassion, and sensitivity. "Every sign of unjust discrimination in their regard should be avoided. These persons are called to fulfill God's will in their lives and, if they are Christians, to unite to the sacrifice of the Lord's Cross the difficulties they may encounter from their condition" (C 2358).

Review Questions

Does the Sixth Commandment only concern adultery?
Explain sexuality in its relation to God.
Who is called to chastity?
Explain the psychology of sin.
What is the difference between adultery and fornication?
Why is "living together" a grave sin?
Does the Church condemn homosexuals?
What does the Church expect of both heterosexual and
    homosexual?

VII. The Seventh Commandment

You shall not steal.

Ex 20 15

The seventh commandment forbids the unjust taking or keeping of another's goods and wronging that person in any way in respect to those goods. On the positive side it demands respect for the goods of another, restoration of goods unjustly taken, or reparation for their value. This commandment is rooted in justice and charity. Beyond actual theft itself, the commandment involves social justice and the social doctrine of the Church.

Theft is taking another's property against the reasonable will of the owner. Deliberate retention of borrowed goods, failing to make restitution for losing the goods of another, business fraud, paying unjust wages, raising prices to take advantage of the hardship or needs of another are all species of theft that demand reparation.

The integrity of creation. Although God gave mankind dominion over creation, this is not an absolute right because the earth and what it contains was destined for the common good of all and succeeding generations. The dominion God bestowed is limited by the quality of life of others and of generations to come. People of "have" nations are required by justice and charity to assist those of "have-not" nations.

Animals are God's creatures, given into the custody of human creation; they are not to be abused or ill-used. There are some people today who equate animal rights with human rights but this is an imbalance not in accord with Scripture which records that humanity was given dominion over all other living things (Gn 1:26). Since the beginning, people used animals for food and clothing, as aids in their labors, and even as companions. Medical experimentation on animals within reasonable limits is morally permissible as long as it is done to save human lives. The Catechism (2418) tells us, "It is contrary to human dignity to cause animals to suffer or die needlessly. . . . One can love animals; one should not direct to them the affection due only to persons."

Preferential Option for the Poor

Both the Old and New Testaments show God's concern and love for the poor. The law of Moses directed attention to the poor: "Since there will never cease to be some in need on the earth, I therefore command you, 'Open your hand to the poor and needy neighbor in your land' " (Deut 15:11). The prophets railed against those who exploited the poor and showed particular concern for widows and orphans.

Jesus identified Himself with the poor and needy, and revealed that our final judgment will be a social one, rooted in the corporal works of mercy: "As you did it not to one of the least of these, you did it not to me" (Mt 25:31-46). One of the saddest moments in the Gospels is when the young man seeking perfection turns away from Jesus "for he had great possessions" (Mt 19:16-23), and Jesus sums up the encounter, "Truly I tell you, it will be hard for a rich person to enter the kingdom of heaven." There is no greater condemnation of the selfish rich than the tirade of St. James (Jas 5:1-6), which begins, "Come now, you rich, weep and howl for the miseries that are coming upon you."

The Church holds up to its children the corporal and spiritual works of mercy as models for their behavior and guides in behalf of others in physical or spiritual need:

Corporal Works of Mercy	*Spiritual Works of Mercy*
1. feeding the hungry	1. counseling the doubtful
2. giving drink to the thirsty	2. instructing the ignorant
3. clothing the naked	3. admonishing sinners
4. visiting the imprisoned	4. comforting the afflicted
5. sheltering the homeless	5. forgiving offenses
6. visiting the sick	6. bearing wrongs patiently
7. burying the dead	7. praying for the living and the dead

The matter of social justice is not only for individuals but exists also on the national and international levels. On the national level the State is responsible for public services and the welfare of its people. It must create a business climate conducive to growth by protecting the rights of those who produce and those who labor in production. Access to employment without discrimination and the payment of a just wage that allows for a dignified livelihood for the worker and family are duties of the State. The State must also provide material welfare for needy citizens while at the same time guarding that welfare does not become a way of life for those who are not aged or ill.

Social justice exists also on the international level. Rich nations have a moral responsibility to developing or underdeveloped countries to see that they are not exploited and are aided in development. Moral considerations must govern relationships between countries and regions, not solely economics. The Church insists that moral doctrine be applied especially in agricultural matters because particularly in the Third World peasants form the overwhelming majority of the poor.

Review Questions

What does the Seventh Commandment forbid?
Explain the notion "the integrity of creation."
What rights do animals have in light of Genesis 1:26?
Explain the Church's preferential option for the poor.
Name the seven corporal works of mercy.
Name the seven spiritual works of mercy.
Discuss the Church's teaching on social justice.

VIII. The Eighth Commandment

You shall not bear false witness
against your neighbor.

Ex 20:16

"This commandment forbids misrepresenting the truth in our relations with others" (C 2464). We are made in the image of God and must bear witness to God who is truth and wills the truth. Scripture tells us that we must serve God in sincerity and truth (Jos 24:14). Truth is necessary for the right conduct of human affairs for as St. Thomas Aquinas tells us, "Men could not live with one another if there were not mutual confidence that they were being truthful with one another." We prove truthfulness not only in our words but also by our deeds, avoiding duplicity, dissimulation, and hypocrisy.

Jesus told Pilate (Jn 18:37) that He came into the world "to bear witness to the truth," and He gave His life in proof of truth. From that time on, from the witness of the deacon Stephen, down to our own day, Christians have given their lives as witnesses to truth. The Church holds up these martyrs as models for our lives, so that in our daily doings we too can always give witness to truth.

Offenses to Truth

St. Augustine tells us that "A *lie* consists of speaking a falsehood with the intention of deceiving." A lie is not the work of God but the work of Satan, whom Jesus called "the father of lies" (Jn 8:44). The purpose of a lie is to lead another into error. The gravity of a lie rests in the degree of harm or injury it does to another. A lie told without malice (what is sometimes referred to as "a white lie") is opposed to this commandment but its gravity is usually that of a venial sin.

Perjury is a lie told under oath. It takes on a particular gravity because it calls upon God to witness an untruth. Perjury contributes to the "condemnation of the innocent, exoneration of the guilty, or the increased punishment of the accused" (C 2476), and hence also takes on the added sin of injustice by compromising judicial decisions and doing an injustice and injury to another. The civil gravity of perjury is found in penal punishment.

Because we are made in the image of God, every person has the right to respect for and honor of his or her reputation. This honor and respect prohibits any attitude or word that would cause unjust injury in this regard. Sins against the reputation of another are:

— *Rash judgment*, assuming as true, without sufficient evidence, the moral fault of another; Jesus condemned needless judgments, warning, "Do not judge, so that you may not be judged" (Mt 7:1);

— *Detraction*, revealing without a valid reason the faults or failings of another to a person who did not know them; this type of gossip often rises from pride, making ourselves seem better than the other person;

— *Calumny*, a remark contrary to the truth which harms the reputation of another. This is a sin against the Eighth Commandment and against justice.

The gravity of the three sins is in proportion to the seriousness of the charge and the damage done. These sins require reparation because they offend against justice and charity, and this reparation obliges in conscience.

Review Questions

What does the Eighth Commandment concern?
What is a lie?
How do we judge the gravity of a lie?
What are some sins against a person's reputation?
Differentiate between calumny and detraction.

IX. The Ninth Commandment

You shall not covet your neighbor's wife.

Ex 20:17

Catholics and Protestants number the commandments differently. Protestants make two commandments out of what is the First Commandment for Catholics, and make one out of what are the Ninth and Tenth Commandments for Catholics. The end results are the same, each division covering the same regulations. Catholics divide what is the Tenth Commandment for Protestants because while each concerns another's possessions, one part of the commandment involves a sexual union that is opposed to the virtue of purity and in violation of a marriage right. This part of the commandment has a relationship with the Catholic Sixth Commandment. The rest of the commandment (the Catholic Tenth Commandment) concerns a neighbor's material possessions and has a connection with the Seventh Commandment.

Both commandments refer to the internal sin of covetousness, or a desire for what one does not possess and which belongs to another. It is a capital sin because it leads to other sins. Covetousness arises out of concupiscence, an inordinate desire for things, which human nature inherited as a result of Adam's fall. As noted earlier, sin begins as an internal act of the intellect, which justifies some deed as good, and thus presents it to the will for action. While covetousness is an internal sin, the danger is that it will become an external action.

Many people are under the impression that if one only thinks about something wrong, it is not wrong unless one does the action. This attitude is incorrect and opposed to the teaching of Christ. Jesus went beyond the act of actual adultery to warn, "I say to you that everyone who looks at a woman lustfully has already committed adultery with her in his heart" (Mt 5:28). Jesus also told us that out of the heart "come evil thoughts, murder, adultery, fornication, theft, false witness, slander" (Mt 15:19).

Thus evil thoughts must be resisted as much as an evil act. Those people who deliberately seek out immoral entertainment or who bring risqué and immoral videocassettes into the home, so that they can be stimulated with mental morose delights, are violating the virtue of *purity*. In the Beatitudes Jesus promised, "Blessed are the pure in heart, for they shall see God" (Mt 5:8). There are two senses to the virtue of purity: In a general sense it refers to a detachment from whatever may lead to sin, an avoidance of all venial sin, and of any willful resistance to grace. In this sense we speak of purity of heart or purity of intention. In a specific sense (and this refers to the Ninth Commandment), purity is the observance of chastity according to one's state in life.

St. John tells us that those who hope to see God must purify themselves for God Himself is pure (1 Jn 3:3). We either purify ourselves in this life or, if we die without grave sin, in the purification of purgatory. We purify ourselves in this life by prayer and meditation, by living a life of chastity, by purity of intention which seeks God as our true end, and by a purity of vision that disciplines the feelings and imagination that would lead us from the path that leads to God.

All of this also requires the virtue of *modesty*. Modesty is the virtue of temperance in one's personal life, in habits, attitudes, speech, dress, etc. The virtue has a certain relativity depending upon place, time, and circumstance. Thus what is permissible in a lay person is not necessarily permissible in a cleric; or what is permissible to a husband and wife is not necessarily allowed an engaged couple; what is permissible in one culture may not be permissible in another.

Review Questions

What does "covet" mean?
What is the difference between external and internal sins?

What does Jesus teach about internal sins?
Why is covetousness called a capital sin?
What are the two meanings of purity?
What does modesty entail?
Explain the relationship of the Sixth and Ninth
   Commandments.

X. The Tenth Commandment

You shall not covet your neighbor's house; . . . or male or female
slave, or ox, or donkey, or anything that belongs to your neighbor.

Ex 20:17

The Tenth Commandment completes the Ninth which is
concerned with concupiscence of the flesh. The Tenth forbids
coveting the goods of another, whether those goods are
material or immaterial. The coveting of material goods is also
an offense against the Seventh Commandment. This
commandment is concerned with the intentions of the heart,
and in effect summarizes all the other commandments. There
is a distinction between covetousness and desire. It is not
unjust to desire something of one's neighbor that can be
acquired by legitimate means, e.g., buying the product of his
garden or his used car. Only when desire goes beyond
reasonable limits does it become covetousness.

Sins against the Tenth Commandment include:

— *Greed,* or the desire to amass earthly goods without
limit. Greed can lead to many injustices: an employer who
pays low wages so that his profit will be greater; a lawyer who
runs up probate fees against an estate contrary to the best
interest of heirs; a doctor who charges Medicare for services
not really rendered; a mechanic who makes unnecessary
repairs; a merchant who raises prices because of a temporary
shortage; a repair man who takes advantage of another's
ignorance in order to cheat him or her, etc.

— *Avarice* is the inordinate desire for temporal goods.
Avarice makes goods and wealth ends in themselves. Avarice
is so occupied with material things that it deadens the just
desire for spiritual things. It ignores the obligations of justice
and charity, and leads to sins of a more serious nature. It

causes unjust methods for acquiring wealth. Jesus pronounced one of His "woes" against the unjust rich (Lk 6:24), and what is sad about many rich is that they do not consider themselves rich but people simply in need of more.

— *Envy* is the sadness at the good of another. It is one of the capital sins that leads to other sins. Envy caused Cain to murder his brother Abel (Gn 4:4-5). Envy leads to the desire to acquire another's goods, even unjustly. St. Augustine called envy "the diabolical sin" for the reasons St. Gregory the Great explained: "From envy are born hatred, detraction, calumny, joy caused by the misfortune of a neighbor, and displeasure caused by his prosperity." Envy is often caused by pride and exaggerated self-esteem.

We prevent these sins by becoming "poor in spirit," as Jesus told us (Mt 5:3).

Review Question

What does the Tenth Commandment forbid?
Explain its relationship to the Seventh Commandment.
Explain the difference between avarice and greed.
Why is envy a capital sin?
How do we guard against sins opposed to the Tenth
    Commandment?

11. The Prayer Life of the Church

Apart from the formal prayer life of the Catholic Church, which is expressed through the sacramental Liturgy, there are other means of grace granted through the Church and rising from the piety of the faithful. These forms have developed over the almost two thousand years of Catholicism as means to give honor to God and work towards the sanctification of the people of God. There are two main forms of such expression: sacramentals and popular devotions.

Sacramentals

Canon law (1166) defines sacramentals as "sacred signs by which spiritual effects especially are signified and are obtained by the intercession of the Church." Sacramentals have been called "little sacraments" but this can be misleading. While there is a resemblance to the sacraments, particularly in the use of a sign, there is also a big difference: grace comes directly through the sacrament by the power of the sacrament itself (*ex opere operato*), while through a sacramental, grace comes indirectly through the intercession of the Church (*ex opere operantis*). The sacramentals draw their power from the Paschal mystery of the passion, death, and resurrection of Christ (C 1670). Sacramentals always include a prayer and usually a specific sign such as the Sign of the Cross, the laying on of hands, or the sprinkling with holy water.

Blessings

The most common form of sacramentals is found in blessings. The Church authorizes a big volume, *The Book of Blessings*, which contains blessings for all sorts of things — an automobile, a new house, an animal, a new mother, people going on a journey. There are blessings of persons, places, objects, meals. As the Congregation for Divine Worship says,

"There is scarcely any proper use of material things which cannot be thus directed toward the sanctification of people and the praise of God." A blessing is made in the name of Jesus and is ordinarily accompanied by the Sign of the Cross.

There are certain formal blessings, found in liturgical rituals, which are part of the ceremonial life of the Church. Among these are the dedication of a church or altar, the blessing of chalices and ciboria, bells, holy oils. Formal blessings or dedication can impart a sacred character to the object blessed, and hence must be treated with respect. Canon law 1171 specifies that sacred things which are to be used in divine worship (particularly chalices, ciboria, and monstrances) are to be treated with reverence and not be employed for profane or improper use even when under control of private individuals. Such usage can be sacrilegious.

Certain sacramentals — consecrations, dedications, blessings — are restricted to a bishop, priest, or deacon. Only a bishop can bless a new church, bells, a cornerstone, a new cemetery, or give a papal blessing. Some sacramentals can be administered by lay people, e.g., signing with ashes on Ash Wednesday, a blessing of a child by a parent, blessing of a meal.

Exorcism

When the Church asks "publicly and authoritatively in the name of Jesus Christ that a person or object be protected against" (C 1673) the power of Satan and withdrawn from his dominion, it is called exorcism (from Greek *exorkizein*, bind with an oath). Jesus performed exorcisms and gave this power to His Apostles (Mk 16:17). Exorcisms are either simple or solemn. A simple exorcism is performed in baptism and in the blessing of Holy Water. A solemn exorcism can only be done by a priest who has been authorized by the bishop.

Solemn exorcisms can only be done after extensive investigation. Illness, particularly mental illness, is not the object of exorcism but a matter for medical science, and must be ruled out before an exorcism can take place. The priest, who is authorized for a particular exorcism must be a man of great prudence and holiness, well acquainted with and strictly observing the rules laid down by the Church (canon 1172). In the matter of exorcisms, the Church wishes to walk between two extremes, those who see demonic influence in any type of bizarre behavior and those who assert that demonic possession never takes place. The Church's experience in this regard extends through almost two millennia and its action in an exorcism is done privately and without publicity.

It is said that Satan's greatest success is in persuading people that he does not exist. Nevertheless, Satan is a reality in Scripture from Genesis 3 on, full of hatred for God and desirous to lead others away from salvation and Jesus Christ. As St. John tells us (1 Jn 3:8), "Everyone who commits sin is a child of the devil; for the devil has been sinning since the beginning. The Son of God was revealed for this purpose, to destroy the works of the devil." Jesus spoke frequently of Satan and his power, and on one occasion He said, "I watched Satan fall from heaven like a flash of lightning." People may not wish to think about Satan, but he is a reality.

Holy Water

One of the strange accusations sometimes leveled against the Church is that Catholics believe that Holy Water has magical powers. Holy water is a sacramental blessed by a priest to ask God's blessing on those who use it. The use of water in ritual goes back to the Old Testament Jews. Water in a way was a Jewish sacramental. Jews washed up to their elbows before eating; returning from a neighboring land, they washed their feet to purify themselves from foreign dust. In 2 Kings 5 we read of the pagan general Naaman who at the bidding of Elisha washed in the Jordan River and was cured of his leprosy. Jesus told a man born blind to go to the pool of Siloam and wash to regain his sight (Jn 9:7).

Holy Water has no magical properties but it is a symbol of purification and a prayer for God's protection. Catholics entering church dip their fingers in the holy water font inside the door and bless themselves as a remembrance of their baptism and as a sign of asking God to purify them of their failings and make their prayer worthy. The rite called the Asperges (sprinkling) takes place in many churches on Sunday as a preparation for Mass. The priest goes through the church sprinkling the congregation with holy water to prepare the people by penance and again as a reminder of their baptism. Catholics also keep blessed water at home and use it at various times (e.g., during a lightning storm) to ask God's protection on their home.

Liturgy of the Hours

Although the celebration of the Eucharist is the central act of daily worship for the Church, prayer of the Liturgy of the Hours is meant to sanctify the various parts of the day, beginning from early morning to late evening. While priests are obliged to recite this prayer daily, the Catholic faithful are also invited to join in, particularly for Laudes (early morning) and Vespers (early evening) as "the two hinges on which the daily Office turns" (General Instruction). The Office is made up of the 150 psalms (distributed over a four-week cycle), canticles, versicles, and antiphons, plus readings from Sacred Scripture and the writings of the Fathers, hymns, and intercessory prayers for the Church and its people.

The Office is also divided into Solemnities and Feasts, and the Memorials of the saints which follow the annual Church calendar. The various seasons of the liturgical year are also observed. In many religious houses the Office is sung or recited as a communal celebration.

Through the Office, the Church follows the command of the Lord to pray without ceasing, and thus daily gives praise to God and intercedes for the salvation of the world.

Veneration of Saints, Images, and Relics

Catholics are frequently accused by those who do not know their Church of worshiping saints (particularly the Virgin Mary), adoring statues (images), and having a superstitious regard for relics. None of these statements are true and everyone of them is a violation of the First

Commandment which binds every Catholic as it does every other Christian. Worship and adoration belong solely to God and to give worship or adoration to anyone else but God is idolatry. The Church teaches that superstition is a sin against the virtue of religion, attributing to some object or person powers that belong solely to God.

What Catholics do give to saints, images, and relics is veneration, the same veneration patriotic Americans give to George Washington or Abraham Lincoln, to whom we erect statues and monuments, and celebrate a holiday in their honor. We honor relics of national heros by enshrining them in museums like the Smithsonian where visitors can see personal objects belonging to persons admired by Americans.

Even so, some fundamentalists will still argue that the Bible condemns the making and use of images. This is not exactly true. What the Bible condemns is the making of idols, images of false gods. In the Lord's instruction to Moses for the building of the Ark of the Covenant, the Jews were instructed to fashion two cherubim (angels) of gold (Ex 25:18). Again in building his great Temple, Solomon had two enormous angels carved for the sanctuary (1 Kgs 6:23) and he engraved the Temple walls with angels, palm trees, and flowers (1 Kgs 6:29). Solomon was not condemned for this but later when his foreign wives imported their pagan idols and Solomon built shrines to such terrible idols as Astarte and Moloch (1 Kgs 11), God became angry with Solomon and promised Solomon's heirs would be stripped of the kingdom because of his idolatry. The biblical distinction between images and idols is very clear.

"But Catholics pray to their images," some will counter. Catholics do not pray to a statue or a picture; they pray to the person whom the statue or picture represents. Statues and images are visual aids that the Church has been using from its beginning. In the Roman catacombs one finds early carvings and frescos that gave visualization to faith. When the Church emerged from the catacombs, it decorated its churches with mosaics, paintings, and statues of religious subjects to aid its people in prayer. Over the centuries, the greatest artists have turned to religious subjects to express their own faith and to strengthen the faith of others.

Popular Catholic Devotions

In addition to the liturgical and sacramental life of Catholics, the faith of the people is nourished by popular forms of piety that arise from their own devotion. These varied forms of prayer supplement the liturgical life. Some of these popular expressions of piety follow.

Devotion to Mary

Of all the saints to whom Catholics render devotion none receives greater veneration, more honor, and respect than Mary, the Mother of Jesus. As pointed out earlier, this disturbs some outside the Church, but for Catholics their devotion to Mary is merely echoing God's choice of her over all other women to be the mother of His Divine Son. What Eve lost for humanity by her sin, Mary was to restore in consenting to become the mother of Jesus, Savior and Redeemer.

Under the inspiration of the Holy Spirit, Mary prophesied "henceforth all generations will call me blessed" (Lk 1:48). For her complete adherence to the will of God (C 967), for her consent to bear the child Jesus, and for her support in His redemptive work, the Church ranks Mary above all other saints, and teaches that in heaven Mary continues her maternal role in behalf of all her earthly children.

To honor Mary, the Church sets aside liturgical feasts. Under one of her liturgical titles, the Immaculate Conception, Mary has been named patroness of the United States. From the moment of her conception, by God's power Mary was kept free from any attachment to sin, including original sin, so that the Angel Gabriel could hail her as "full of grace" (Lk 1:28). Every day every priest recites as part of the Divine Office the Magnificat prayer Mary spoke to Elizabeth (Lk 1:46-55). There are other prayers to Mary that the Church encourages its children to say, particularly the prayer known as the Rosary.

The Rosary

The most popular private devotion is the recitation of the Rosary, a word that applies not only to the devotion but also to the string of beads (from Middle English *bede*, a prayer) on which the prayers are counted. Although there are various rosaries the most popular form is that which centers on incidents in the lives of Jesus and Mary, known as the Marian Rosary.

This Rosary consists of five decades of beads, each decade separated by a large bead. On the large bead the Our Father (*Pater Noster*) is recited, followed by ten beads, each a Hail Mary (the Angelic Salutation), with a Glory Be to the Father (*Gloria Patri*) concluding each decade. While the prayers are being said, the person meditates on the mystery of the decade.

These mysteries are:

JOYFUL MYSTERIES
1. The Annunciation
2. Visit to Elizabeth
3. The Nativity
4. Presentation in the Temple
5. Finding the Boy Jesus

SORROWFUL MYSTERIES
1. Agony in the Garden
2. Scourging at the Pillar
3. Crowning With Thorns
4. Carrying the Cross
5. The Crucifixion

GLORIOUS MYSTERIES
1. The Resurrection
2. The Ascension
3. Descent of the Holy Spirit
4. The Assumption
5. Crowning of Mary

The Marian Rosary is a beloved devotion because it leads the person at prayer through the joys, sorrows, and glory that touched the lives of Jesus and Mary. It can be said privately anywhere and when said in common it is a communion of prayer with other Christians that is neither tiresome nor repetitious.

Stations of the Cross

Also called the Way of the Cross, this devotion first became popular in the late Middle Ages among people who could not go on pilgrimage to the Holy Land. Depictions of fourteen scenes in the passion of Jesus are mounted on the walls of the church or chapel and the person goes from one to another meditating upon the incident represented. If the devotion is communal, only the leader goes from station to station.

The stations are: 1. Jesus is condemned to death; 2. Jesus takes up His Cross; 3. Jesus falls the first time; 4. Jesus meets His mother; 5. Simon of Cyrene helps Jesus; 6. Veronica wipes the face of Jesus; 7. the second fall; 8. Jesus meets the women of Jerusalem; 9. the third fall; 10. Jesus is stripped of His garments; 11. Jesus is nailed to the Cross; 12. Jesus dies on the Cross; 13. Jesus is taken down from the Cross; 14. Jesus is buried in the tomb.

Because some of these stations are based on popular piety and not Scripture (e.g., the three falls, Veronica), Pope John Paul II introduced Gospel stations on Good Friday, 1991. These stations are: 1. The agony in the garden; 2. Jesus betrayed by Judas and arrested; 3. condemned by Sanhedrin; 4. denied by Peter; 5. condemned by Pilate; 6. scourged and crowned with thorns; 7. Jesus carries His Cross; 8. Simon of Cyrene aids Jesus; 9. Jesus meets women of Jerusalem; 10. Jesus is crucified; 11. the repentant thief; 12. Jesus speaks to His mother; 13. Jesus dies on the Cross; 14. the burial. It is too early to tell if these new stations will replace the traditional ones.

Pilgrimages

Another expression of Catholic devotion is in pilgrimages; these are journeys, alone or in a group, to a shrine for a religious purpose (e.g., to fulfill a promise, as an act of worship, to seek spiritual aid, as an act of penance). In the early days, pilgrims came to Rome to pray at the tombs of Peter and Paul. Holy Land pilgrimages were popular but were often hindered by Moslem restrictions. In the Middle Ages, the tomb of St. James at Santiago de Compostela in Spain attracted pilgrims from all over Europe.

Today the most popular places for pilgrimages in North America are the Shrine of Our Lady of Guadalupe in Mexico City; the Shrine of the North American Martyrs in Auriesville, N.Y.; and in Canada, the Basilica of St. Joseph in Montreal and the Shrine of St. Anne in Quebec. In Europe, Rome is still a major center for pilgrimages, followed by Lourdes in France and Fatima in Portugal, where Pope John Paul II went on pilgrimage after the attempt on his life. Many countries have national pilgrimage centers, some of which attract pilgrims from other lands, e.g., Our Lady of Czestochowa in Poland which was the heart of Polish resistance to Communism.

Many of these places of pilgrimage have the reputation for miracles being worked there. A *miracle* is an observable effect in the moral or spiritual order which is in contravention of natural laws and cannot be explained by any natural power but only by the power of God. Miracles are required for canonization. The Church only admits a miracle when every natural explanation is cxhausted. At Lourdes a medical bureau examines each purported cure and it is only a rare one that is listed as miraculous.

Some Other Devotions

— *Relics.* The Church venerates its relics (L. *reliquiae*, remains). Relics are divided into three classes. A first-class relic is the body of a saint or any part of it. A second-class relic is any object intimately connected with the saint, such as a Bible or Breviary. A third class relic is anything touched to the body of a saint. The Church also takes great care of its relics. Canon law 1190 states: "It is absolutely forbidden to sell sacred relics. Significant relics or other ones which are honored with great veneration by the people cannot in any manner be validly alienated or perpetually transferred without the permission of the Apostolic See."

The veneration of relics is often misunderstood by those outside the Church. One hears such charges as, "If all the wood of the True Cross relics was put together it would make a forest" or the question, "How can the same relic exist in several places?" Except for a few large pieces, most of the relics of the True Cross are but slivers, which if gathered together would only make a few cupfuls. Also, there are three pillars of the Scourging, one each in Rome, Constantinople, and Jerusalem, but, when examined, it is readily seen that each is only a piece of a pillar. Many relics are divided for wider veneration. Relics are ordinarily preserved in a reliquary, often fashioned like a small monstrance, usually displayed for public veneration on the saint's feast day.

— *Medals*. A medal is a flat metal disk bearing the image of Our Lord, Mary, some holy person, or a mystery of religion It can be blessed by the Church. Wearers of medals are warned by the Church to guard against superstition and to use the medal only to honor the image represented and as a reminder of the need for advancing in Christian perfection.

— *Images*. These are paintings, sculptures, carvings, or other representations of Our Lord, Our Lady, a saint, or some other holy representation. When such images are used in church decoration, the Constitution on the Liturgy of Vatican Council II said that they should be of high artistic value and avoid sentimentality. As noted earlier, images are venerated not for themselves but for what they represent.

All of these forms of giving honor to God reveal the richness of the prayer life of Catholics, which goes beyond the Sunday worship. They are the result of the long experience of the Catholic Church of leading its people in diverse ways to God. While the Eucharist is the central and supreme worship of the Church, these other forms give rise to individual expressions of faith and as such are guarded and regulated by the Church.

Review Questions

Explain the difference between a sacrament and a
    sacramental.
Name some sacramentals.
What is said to be Satan's greatest success?
Does the Bible justify the use of holy water?

Who is obliged to say the Liturgy of the Hours? What about
  the laity?
Explain the difference between worship and veneration.
Do Catholics worship Mary? Explain.
What does the biblical condemnation of images mean?
Do Catholics pray to statues?
What is the most popular Catholic devotion?
What is a miracle?
Why do Catholics venerate relics?
What must one guard against in wearing a medal or
  practicing a devotion?

12. Non-Christian Religions

Thou hast made us for Thyself, O Lord,
and our hearts are restless until they rest in Thee.

St. Augustine, *Confessions*

In his *Soliloquies (387)*, reflecting on his early dissolute life
and his search for God, St. Augustine wrote, "I was wandering
like a lost sheep, searching outside of myself for that which
was within. I ran through all the streets and squares of this
great city, the world, searching for Thee, O God, and I found
Thee not, because I sought Thee wrongly. Thou wert within
me and I sought Thee without."

What Augustine discovered is that within each person is a
desire for God but it is a desire that without the aid of grace
can be totally perverted into atheism; twisted into a hedonism
that can make a god of money, power, or self. When a person
follows the desire, it becomes a religion, a word that is difficult
to define. Catholics would define religion as the moral virtue
which inclines a person to give due reverence and worship to
God. But there are recognized religions that give worship to
many gods; Hinduism is an example. There are also
recognized religions that worship no god, such as Buddhism
or Taoism, which more or less correspond to the ethical
culture of the West. There is also animism which finds souls
in grass and trees and draws its gods from nature. The
variations go on and on.

While all humans have a desire for God buried somewhere
within, history has shown that mistakes are usually the rule
in trying to interpret that desire. While all religions share to a
greater or lesser degree in Truth, without God's help, God
Himself will not be found. God has revealed Himself to
mankind, yet only three religions share in that revelation:
Christianity (which this book has been describing), Judaism,
and Islam. These are the three monotheistic religions that
recognize only one God, who is creator and legislator. While
the self-revelation of that one God began at the creation of
humanity, it became distorted as the result of original sin.

Judaism teaches, and Christianity and Islam accept, that

God renewed revelation of Himself through Abraham and the prophets who descended from his line. The Church teaches that this revelation came to fulfillment in Jesus Christ with whom revelation ended. Islam, on the other hand, holds that God's revelation continued through Muhammad, the founder of Islam, who was the last of the prophets.

A description of these two great monotheistic religions follows.

Judaism

History. Historians are divided on assigning a date when Judaism began. Some see its origin in Abraham (whom the Catholic Church calls "our father in faith" [Eucharistic Prayer I]). Others put it at the conquest of Palestine, fourteenth century BC onward. Still others assign its beginning to the sixth century BC when the Palestinian exiles, mostly of the tribe of Judah (Ezra 1 and 2) returned from Babylonian exile. Nevertheless, there is a continuity to the Jewish people from Abraham on. Abraham was called by God to leave his home in Ur of the Chaldeans (Mesopotamia) and resettle in distant Palestine. For his obedience Abraham, an aged and childless man, was given a son, Isaac, who in turn had two sons, Esau and Jacob.

By trickery, Jacob succeeded as heir of Isaac. Jacob had twelve sons, founders of the twelve tribes of Israel, a name given by God to Jacob, which also became a collective name for his descendants. Joseph, one of Jacob's sons, was sold by his brothers into Egyptian slavery, but Joseph rose to become a powerful figure in the Egyptian government. When a terrible famine struck Palestine, Joseph brought all his family to the safety of Egypt. In time, the descendants of Israel became Egyptian slaves. God chose Moses to rescue His chosen people and lead them back to Palestine, who once there sought a king to lead them. Saul became Israel's first kingly failure and was succeeded by David and then his son, Solomon. In the years that followed the Jews drifted in and out of fidelity to God.

God sent prophets to guide and warn His people but these

prophets often met hostility and persecution by the Jewish leadership. The prophets' warnings came to fulfillment when armies from the north invaded Palestine and carried the Jews off to exile in Assyria and Babylonia. When the Assyrians were defeated by the Persian king, Darius, the new conqueror allowed the Jews to return home, where, under the guidance of the prophet Ezra, Jewish life was restored. In the years that followed, Judaism was attacked by various sources, particularly by advancing Greek hedonism, following the conquest of Alexander the Great. Finally, the nation came under the domination of the Romans until after the death of Jesus, the Jews rose in rebellion. The Romans cruelly put down the revolt, destroyed the Temple and much of Jerusalem, and drove the people into the diaspora where they remained until modern times when Israel was restored as a nation.

Religion. The history and religion of the Jewish people is recorded in the Old Testament. The term "Judaism" is largely of modern usage, as it does not exist in the Bible or in rabbinic literature. Scholars use two terms when describing Judaism: *Torah,* which is the divinely revealed teachings, basically the Ten Commandments; and *Yehudit,* which refers to the laws, customs, and practices which were created by Jewish religious leadership in their interpretation of the Torah. Jesus distinguished between these two sources and was frequently critical of the Jewish leadership of placing too much emphasis on the man-made laws to the detriment of the divine law. Jews believe themselves to be the people of God and in varying ways attempt to live His Law. However, many Jews today are but secular Jews — Jews by blood but not by belief.

Judaism was divided into sects at the time of Christ and is even more divided today. The Temple was replaced by the synagogue (although some modern Jews refer to the synagogue as temple) and the Jewish priesthood by the rabbinate, and the ceremony of sacrifices by prayer and study. The repository of the Oral Law (Talmud) produced great commentators like Rashi and Maimonides, and more modern Judaism such teachers as Elijah ben Solomon and Moses

Mendelssohn, who influence Jewish thought to this day. Regionalism also influenced Jewish development as the Shepardic, Marranos, and national movements developed. Today Judaism goes from ultraliberalism to ultraconservatism — Reformed Jews to Hasidic, with Conservative and Orthodox occupying the more central positions. There is also a renewed Messianism, particularly among the Hasidim. A modern Jew, when asked to describe his religion, answered in three words: "God, Torah, Israel."

Practices. While all Jews recognize the Sabbath (sundown Friday to sundown Saturday) and the holy days, particularly Passover, Yom Kippur (Day of Atonement), and Rosh Hashanah (New Year), Jews differ widely in their practices of religion. All religious Jews have their sons go through the Bar Mitzvah ceremony when they reach the age of thirteen in which the young male is initiated into the religious community, reading publicly in the synagogue from the Torah. Reform and Conservative Jews, yielding to female pressures, have established a similar ceremony (Bat Mitzvah) for girls.

Strict observance of the Sabbath with synagogue attendance is practiced by many Jews, while others are never seen in the synagogue except for high holy days. Some Jews keep very strict daily prayer practices, while others save prayer for the synagogue. Some Jews keep very kosher (ritually fit for use) households, use only kosher foods (prepared under rabbinical supervision), avoid banned foods (pork, shellfish, etc.), keeping two sets of dishes (one for dairy products), and so on. Some Jewish males (particularly Hasidim) are never seen in public without a hat covering the hair, and usually with a beard, while others wear only a small skull cap (yarmulke) in the synagogue, and still other males cannot be distinguished in any way from goyim (gentiles). Christians who entertain Jews should be sensitive to their guests' preferences. Over the centuries the Jews have been persecuted for their beliefs and "differences." Christians must remember that we are all descendants of the same spiritual father (Abraham) who gave us our belief in the One God, that

Christianity grew out of Judaism, and that the founders of our religion were Jews, as were all the early Christians.

Islam

Islam (Arabic, submission to God), the third monotheistic religion, is a religion centered in its members' adherence to the will of Allah (the Arabic word for God) as revealed to Muhammad, a camel driver, and recorded by him in the Muslim Bible known as the Koran (Quran), Arabic, meaning "the reading." The first verse of the book begins "Read! Read in the name of your Lord who created man." It is a book that was written over most of Muhammad's adult lifetime and was strongly influenced by his caravan travels where he came into contact with Judaism, Christianity, and Gnosticism. Muhammad taught that the Koran was revealed to him by the Angel Gabriel. Muslims accept the Koran as guide for all facets of life. Since the Koran was written in Arabic, this is the language of Islam.

Muslims look upon Muhammad as the final and greatest of the prophets. Other prophets that Muslims accept are Adam, Noah, Abraham, Moses, and Jesus. Abraham was the first Muslim. Jesus was born of the Virgin Mary and did great miracles. He was not crucified but taken away by God, who left a shadow in his place (Gnosticism). He will return as Messiah at the end of the world to fight the Anti-Christ. Since Muhammad lived in Mecca (today in Saudi Arabia) and the religion was founded there c. AD 620, Muslims consider Mecca the center of their religion and pray each day facing Mecca. Friday is the Muslim holy day, the month of Ramadan, the Muslim Lent. In this month Muslims do not eat between dawn and dusk. Muslims on the whole are very faithful to their religious duties, observing the five pillars of Islam: 1. Proclaiming with understanding and acceptance, "There is no god but Allah and Muhammad is His prophet"; 2. Offering the five daily prayers (dawn, noon, midafternoon, sunset, evening), kneeling and bowed in the direction of the holy city of Mecca (on Friday the noon prayer is said in the mosque); 3.

Giving alms to the poor and needy; 4. Fasting during Ramadan; 5. Joining at least one pilgrimage (*hajj*) to Mecca.

One should not gather that Islam is monolithic for outside of the five pillars there are many theological disagreements and a large number of sects. The two main divisions are the Sunni, which claims orthodoxy and which has given birth to only one main sect, the Wahhabis; and the Shiites, who have departed from the original Islam, and have given birth to numerous sects. While Islam has its rituals, it does not have a priesthood, and its members are served by imams (prayer leaders) and muzzeins (summoners to prayer). Although Muslims are divided theologically and politically, there are areas of agreement: injunctions against alcoholic drinks, the touching or eating of pork, usury, and the making of images, which led Muslim artists to develop highly skilled calligraphy and intricate line designs. Muslims produced highly skilled geographers and mathematicians, and to them the West owes its Arabic system of numbers.

Islam was spread through the sword (*jihad*, holy war), and its first-century growth was phenomenal. It moved from Arabia up into the Middle East, across North Africa, into Asia and the South Pacific islands. Muslims conquered Spain, the Balkans and advanced into regions that became Russia. For a time, they threatened the whole of Europe until they were driven from Spain by Ferdinand and Isabella about the time Columbus discovered America; later, Turk invaders were defeated in the Battle of Lepanto (1571).

A number of Islamic countries are today secular states, particularly Turkey and Egypt. However a recent phenomenon is a reawakened fundamentalism which seeks national domination that would conform the country entirely to Islamic law and discipline; Iran is a prime example, but fundamentalism has strong influence in such places as Pakistan, Sudan, and regions of North Africa. Accompanying the growth in fundamentalism has been the spread of Islam through migration. France and the United States have growing Muslim populations. Islam is now the second largest religion in the world (881 million Muslims, compared to 1.7 billion Christians).

Buddhism

Buddhism, both a religion and philosophy, a system without God or gods, was founded in India in the sixth century BC by Siddhartha Gautama, called the Buddha (the Enlightened One). In the life of Gautama it is difficult to separate fact from legend. He is said to have been born in what is now Nepal in the year 563 BC, a noble in a warrior clan. He married and had a son. At the age of twenty-nine he deserted his family and left the palace to seek enlightenment, studying yogic meditation techniques, giving himself up to fasting and austerities. Finally, he seated himself under a fig tree and swore not to leave until he reached enlightenment. On the night of a full moon, after overcoming the temptations of Mara, the evil one, he attained supreme enlightenment and became Buddha at the age of thirty-five. For the next forty-five years he preached his doctrines, gathered disciples, and formed monasteries. He was cremated after death and his ashes given to eight groups of followers.

Buddha formed his teaching into what he called "the four noble truths" and "the eightfold path." The four noble truths are: 1. Existence is suffering; 2. Suffering is caused by craving and attachment; 3. Suffering ends in nirvana, a state of supreme liberation and bliss; 4. One reaches nirvana through the eightfold path. The eightfold path consists of right views, right resolve, right speech, right action, right livelihood, right effort, right mindedness, and right concentration. After the death of Buddha these teachings were written down and expounded upon, forming three schools: Theravada (Sri Lanka, Burma, and Southeast Asia), Mahayana (China, Korea, Japan), and Vajrayana (Tibet). Buddhism is practically extinct today in India, the country of its origin, except for Tibetan refugees. There are sects devolving from these three traditions.

Zen Buddhism is a type of Buddhism popular with some Americans. It is a sect that exists in both China (referred to as Ch'an) and Japan, and takes its name from the Japanese *zen*, meditation. Japanese Zen exists mainly in the Soto sect, which emphasizes sitting in meditation without expectation and with faith in one's own state of enlightenment. Zen Buddhism has strongly influenced Japanese literary and artistic life, finding expression in calligraphy, poetry, tea ceremony, flower arrangement, and sand gardens. Zen Buddhism was brought to the United States after World War II and now has monasteries in various parts of the country that teach its methods of meditation.

Hinduism

Hinduism is a western term used to describe the religious beliefs of the majority of the people of India. It is a very difficult word to pin down because it exists in a variety of forms with a pantheon of gods that seem to rival that of the ancient Roman gods. It is a religion that had no single founder but grew by syncretism over four millennia. There is a great deal of mysticism, mystery, and superstition. The most popular deity is Vishnu; he has incarnations as Krishna and Rama. There is Shiva, the horned god of death and destruction, birth and reproduction, and Shiva's consort, the avenging Kali. All of this is contained in the Hindu sacred book, the Veda.

Traditional Hinduism advocated world renunciation but modern teachers have veered away from this to unite spiritual life with social concern. The various forms of Hinduism center in the doctrine of *karma*, through which the individual reaps a series of lifetimes according to good or bad actions. Implicit in this is the transmigration of souls from one body to another. The goal of the Hindu is the state of *moksha*, liberation from suffering and the compulsion to rebirth. This is attained when the passions have been conquered and is accomplished only by the most devout.

Yoga is a term used in Indian thought. It refers to a type of spiritual discipline that leads to higher consciousness and liberation from suffering and rebirth. There are various systems of yoga, ordinarily practiced under the guidance of a guru (spiritual guide). One popular yoga system in this country is concentration on a mantra which is repeated over and over. Sometimes the mantra is a Sanskrit verse, but more often it is a syllable without semantic meaning or the repetition of the name of a Hindu deity. Many Americans became familiar with Hindus of the Krishna sect chanting their mantra on American streets: "Hare Krishna, Hare Krishna, Krishna Krishna, Hare Hare, Hare Rama, Rama Rama, Hare Hare."

Some of these Indian gurus have become rich men in peddling their mysticism to Americans, in founding religious communes and meditation "schools." One of the most successful of these is Maharishi Mahesh Yogi, who came to this country and founded the Spiritual Rejuvenation Movement and today has schools all over the United States that teach a type of yoga called Transcendental Meditation which has attracted millions of Americans to sample Hindu mysticism. That the aim of these gurus is conversion is not to be denied.

The list could go on and on — Baha'i, a Persian heresy of Shiite Islam; Unification Church, while it has a veneer of Christianity, its teaching is more Taoist than Christian; finally, there are the New Age movements, practically all of which combine Eastern mysticism with Western pop psychology.

The Irreligious

Atheism, "since it rejects or denies the existence of God . . , is a sin against the virtue of religion" (C 2125), and is generally rooted in pride. The Bible tells us, "The fool says in his heart, 'There is no God' " (Ps 14:1). Vatican II's Pastoral Constitution on the Church in the Modern World calls atheism "one of the most serious problems of our times" (no. 19). While there were atheists in past times, they were relatively few and were looked upon with disdain and contempt. However, beginning in the nineteenth century, the perceived conflict between religion and science created a new class of God-deniers, who were fed by such preachers of atheism as Ralph Ingersoll. Today atheists are even organized into groups to attack belief in God and use the modern means of communication to promote their negativism.

The Catechism tells us (2124) that the term "atheism" covers different phenomena. "One common form is the practical materialism which restricts its needs and aspirations to space and time." Atheistic humanism falsely considers the individual to be an end to him or herself, and the sole maker, with supreme control, of one's personal history. The early Communists railed against religion as "pie in the sky" because they believed it thwarted social and economic liberation by raising hopes, not to this world but in a future life. Thus the Communists systematically attempted to root God from human life, yet when Communism finally collapsed, it left behind people who were still believers or seekers.

It was noted above that atheism is often rooted in pride which creates a false conception of human autonomy in which the person refuses any dependence on God, making himself an end in itself. Yet, the Catechism tells us "to acknowledge God is in no way to oppose the dignity of man, since such dignity is grounded and brought to perfection in God." Actually, only blinded by pride can the atheist go against the secret desires of his heart.

Agnosticism is a form of skepticism that says the existence of God can neither be proven nor denied. It was T. H. Huxley who coined the word in 1869 and joining him in this suspension of judgment were such writers as Herbert Spencer, Auguste Comte, and Immanuel Kant. Agnosticism has been called practical atheism because in the end the result is the same as atheism. While the agnostic says, "I don't know," that often means, "I don't think so," because to make the statement one has to ignore the Bible, the life, and the teaching of Christ, the Church, and its saints, and imply that they are all wrong in belief in God.

Indifferentism is in effect more offensive to God than either atheism or agnosticism because it refuses to make a decision and regards the existence of God as not important one way or another. In the Book of Revelation, John is directed by the Son of Man to write this warning: "I know your works; you are neither cold nor hot. Would that you were cold or hot! So, because you are lukewarm, and neither cold nor hot, I will spew you out of my mouth." This is God's view of indifferentism.

Indifferentism leads to the vice of amorality which gives rise to "serious errors in the areas of education, politics, social action, and morals" (C 407). This is particularly true in the type of entertainment being offered today. The writers and producers do not set out to be immoral but by their indifference to morality and in their desire to titillate in order to gain rating points, they produce a steady stream of immoral actions and situations. Christians have to be aware of this amorality and reject it. The late theologian and philosopher, Dietrich von Hildebrand, once observed that paganism in some ways is preferable to the secularism of our times. Others have called secularism the new paganism. At the root of secularism is amorality.

Review Questions

Define religion.
What religions share in God's revelation of Himself?
What Jewish belief does Christianity and Islam accept?
How do Judaism, Christianity, and Islam differ from one
    other?
What are the main Jewish holy days?
How do Muslims regard Muhammad?
What are the five pillars of Islam?
How was Islam spread?
Describe Buddhism.
What is Zen Buddhism?
How does Buddhism differ from Hinduism?
Does Hinduism teach reincarnation?
What is the source of Transcendental Meditation?
What is the difference between atheism and agnosticism?
How does God view indifferentism?

13. The Mission of the Catholic

The Catholic Church is missionary by its very nature, since, according to the plan of the Father, it has its origin in the mission of the Son and Holy Spirit. The mission assigned by the Father to the Son was in turn passed on by Him to His Church: "Go into all the world and preach the gospel to the whole creation" (Mk 16:15). St. Paul took this command personally and at one point cried out, "Woe to me if I do not proclaim the Gospel!" (1 Cor 9:16). Pope John Paul II at the beginning of his great encyclical, The Mission of the Redeemer, stressed his own involvement: "In the name of the whole Church, I sense an urgent duty to repeat this cry of St. Paul. From the very beginning of my pontificate I have chosen to travel to the ends of the earth in order to show this missionary concern. My direct contact with the peoples who do not know Christ has convinced me even more of the *urgency of missionary activity.*"

While statistically the number of Catholics increases each year, in actuality, in relation with world population, the proportion of Catholics grows less. There are several billion people, and their number increases daily (since the end of Vatican II it has doubled) who have never heard the teachings of Christ. Catholics for the most part have been content to leave the task of evangelization to those priests, religious brothers and sisters, and lay missioners who have given their lives to this work, supporting them by their aims but taking no part in the direct work of conversion themselves. Although one should not expect all members of the laity to rush off to the ends of the earth, one can expect that they reach out to others in their own environments. One might also expect that they catch some of the fervor and urgency of St. Paul.

The Second Book of the Code of Canon Law is directed towards the laity, the people of God. The very first canon of that book reminds the laity of their obligation in this regard (canon 204):

> Christ's faithful are those who, since they are incorporated into
> Christ through baptism, are constituted the people of God. For this
> reason they participate in their own way in the priestly, prophetic
> and kingly office of Christ. *They are called*, each according to his
> or her particular condition, *to exercise the mission which God
> entrusted to the Church to fulfill in the world.* (Italics mine.)

There are some Christians today who even question the
validity of current missionary work, wondering if it is expected
in this modern age. They admit the need of social action in
behalf of the poor and needy of the world, but question the
value of conversion. Did not the council teach (*Lumen
Gentium*, 16) that those who through no fault of their own do
not know Christ but seek God with a sincere heart can
achieve eternal salvation? Why then should there be
missionary activity?

Missionary activity exists because it is the will of Jesus
who was assigned the mission of salvation on earth and made
by the Father the gateway to heaven. Jesus told His Apostles:
"I am the way, and the truth, and the life; no one comes to the
Father, but by me" (Jn 14:6). Peter, who was arrested for
curing a lame man, told the Sanhedrin that he cured the man
in the name of Jesus Christ, the same Jesus they had
crucified. Peter added, "And there is salvation in no one else,
for there is no other name under heaven given among men by
which we must be saved" (Acts 4:12). As Paul tells us, God's
plan is "to unite all things in Christ, things in heaven and
things on earth." The Church then is in mission because it is
the will of the Father and Son that it should be the ordinary
means of salvation.

The Church exists for the salvation of humanity, not solely
for those born into it. Jesus died for all people of all times.
Since God offers salvation to all, that salvation must be made
available. To the question "why missions?" Pope John Paul
answered in his encyclical, "We reply with the Church's faith
and experience that true liberation consists in opening oneself
to the love of Christ. In Him, and only in Him, are we set free
from all alienation and doubt, from slavery to the power of sin
and death. . . . *Mission is an issue of faith,* an accurate

indicator of our faith in Christ and His love for us." The pope sees mission as a service of Catholics to their brothers and sisters and as a fitting response to God. The simplest answer to "why missions?" is that it is the will of Jesus Christ.

Today the laity can play a greater role in mission than ever before. People today put more trust in witnesses than in teachers. The laity can give the example of Christian living which is more persuasive than theories. As the pope says, "The evangelical witness which the world finds most appealing is that of concern for people, and of charity towards the poor, the weak, and those who suffer. The complete generosity underlying this attitude and these actions stands in marked contrast to human selfishness. It raises precise questions that lead to God and to the Gospel."

This does not mean that there is no need of proclamation, which the Church calls "a permanent priority of mission." It is the mandate of Christ that the Good News be preached. People must be told that they are loved and saved by God through His Son, Jesus Christ, who is our full and authentic liberation from sin, evil, and death. Jesus is the giver of "new life." Paul asked his converts to pray for him, "that utterance may be given me in opening my mouth boldly to proclaim the mystery of the gospel, for which I am an ambassador in chains; that I may declare it boldly, as I ought to speak" (Eph 6:19-50).

The accusation is sometimes made about professionals within the Church that they are "saving the saved." There is some truth in the fact that many are content to maintain the status quo, for it is often easier to build on what one has than to lay new foundations. Nevertheless, it is the mandate of Jesus to "go and make disciples." One does not even have to look beyond the territorial reaches of one's own parish to find the unchurched. On that same priest lies the obligation to provide missionary formation to the people in his care so that they too can take part in the mission of the Church. Teachers, and particularly theologians who teach in seminaries and lay centers, must be animators for mission.

The Church Is Countercultural

The Church of Christ that we must present to the world is a Church that is the opposite of worldly values. "We preach Christ crucified," Paul wrote his converts (1 Cor 1:23), "a stumbling block to Jews and folly to Gentiles." Jesus told us that while we must live in the world, we cannot be of the world. On the night of His arrest, Jesus prayed to His Father for His Apostles: "I have given them thy word; and the world has hated them because they are not of the world, even as I am not of the world" (Jn 17:14).

The Church, faithful to the teachings of Christ, is a sign of contradiction to the world, and for this the Church is vilified. Christians who live opposite to the values of the world are called conservatives, rightists, fanatics, one-dimensional. Nevertheless, the Christian is called to bear witness to Christ by taking courageous and prophetic stands, despite worldly persecution and in the face of its secular political and economic power. The world has moved from a quasi-morality to liberalism and now to permissivism. It aims to show Catholic teaching as unreasonable and that Catholics are on the margin of society. The modern moral theologian to remain credible is asked to compromise his teaching, and some do, but the follower of Christ can no more compromise truth than could the Master.

The essential conflict for the Church today is not with other world religions but with secularism which is diabolic in its message and appeal. The answer is not in philosophical or theological debate but in Jesus Christ Crucified. This is an answer for which the world has no response. In a age when money, power, luxury are goals, Jesus moves in the opposite direction. Jesus is the sign of contradiction that can change the world. What we are to tell the non-Christians of the world is:

> Your attitude must be that of Christ.
> Though he was born in the form of God,
> he did not deem equality with God
> something to be grasped at.
> Rather, he emptied himself

and took the form of a slave,
being born in the likeness of men.
He was known to be of human estate,
and it was thus that he humbled
himself,
obediently accepting even death,
death on a cross.
Because of this,
God highly exalted him
and bestowed on him the name
above every other name.
So that at Jesus' name
every knee must bend
in the heavens, on the earth,
and under the earth,
and every tongue proclaim
to the glory of God the Father:
JESUS CHRIST IS LORD!

Phil 2:5-11; NAB

A Final Word

This book has had a threefold purpose:

1. To show that Jesus Christ founded the Catholic Church and no other;
2. To give evidence that Jesus Christ is central to Catholic life and worship;
3. Finally, to demonstrate that the Catholic Church is a biblical Church, basing its teaching in the Bible.

It is hoped that this book will deepen and better systematize the faith of Catholics and lead any non-Catholics who come across it to examine in greater detail the claim that the Catholic Church is the Church Christ founded and the one to which He wills all should belong.

Review Questions

What is the Great Command of Christ?
How did St. Paul express this?

What does the first canon law on the laity enjoin?
Why are we called to mission?
Why is the Church called "a sign of contradiction"?
What are Christians to tell the non-Christian world?

Index